3₊T 6.62

THEATER BUSINESS

From Auditions through Opening Night

THEATER BUSINESS

FROM AUDITIONS THROUGH OPENING NIGHT

Jan Weingarten Greenberg

HOLT, RINEHART AND WINSTON / NEW YORK

J
792
G

Library of Congress Cataloging in Publication Data
Greenberg, Jan   Theater business.
Bibliography: p.201   Includes index.
Summary: Discusses the steps involved in producing
commercial plays and musicals.
1. Theater—Vocational guidance—Juvenile literature.
2. Theater—United States—New York (City)—Juvenile
literature. [1. Theater—Production and direction]
I. Title.   PN2074.G7   792'.0232   80-20295   ISBN 0-03-051451-7

To Lester—my husband,
Kim, Polly, my parents and sister

I would like to thank the following people whose knowledge, time, concern, and support made this book possible: Shirley Herz, Sam Rudy, Gail Bell, Miriam Chaikin, Patt Dale, Barbara Eliron, Randy Estebrook, Burry Fredrik, Carol Greenberg, Paul Heller, Fritz Holt, David Lawlor, Jacques LeSourd, Dorothy Olim, Mary Saunders, Zoya Wyeth, Gloria Nelson, and Teresa Thompson.

Contents

THEATER BUSINESS

From Auditions through Opening Night

Introduction

In the 1979–80 Broadway season, sixty-three shows opened. Millions of theater-goers spent almost $325 million on tickets for Broadway shows and the national touring companies of Broadway productions. Yet, of the sixty-three shows that opened, as of June 1980 only three had actually made back enough money to repay their production costs.

Probably no other business could continue in a situation where such sums are lost most of the time. Yet the Broadway theater as a business not only survives but thrives. It is a business that involves tremendous sums of money, often more than a million dollars to mount a single production. It employs thousands of people, ranging from the stars whose names are household words to the elderly men who guard the stage door entrances. It is a business in which there are not enough jobs for all the people who want to work; in which unemployment is rampant even in the best of times; and in which the vast majority are thankful just to work and do not think of ever getting rich. The hours are long and family and friends must often be left behind for weeks or months at a time. The Broadway theater is a business that people enter and remain in because they love it.

As in any business, there is a product. In the theater, the

Wednesday, November 19, 1980

Season Boxoffice Totals

(The tabulation below lists the total net boxoffice receipts for Broadway and the road last week and for the corresponding weeks last season, and the seasons of 1970-71 and 1960-61, as well as the number of shows running those respective weeks. In addition, it lists the running total boxoffice receipts for the respective seasons thus far, plus the running total numbers of playing weeks for the corresponding periods of the respective seasons. (E indicates that the figure is estimated).

(24th WEEK OF SEASON)

	This Season	1979-80 Season	1970-71 Season	1960-61 Season
BROADWAY				
Shows Playing Last Week	33	27	24	27
Total Playing Weeks to Date	689	685	423	405
Paid Attendance Last Week	224,426	175,886	---	---
Total Attendance to Date	5,008,944	4,012,063	---	---
Total Receipts Last Week	$3,965,166	$2,713,686	$1,245,429	$937,700
Season Total Receipts to Date	$84,670,444	$59,508,205	$21,305,027	$15,392,700
Average Paid Admission Last Week . . .	$17.67	$15.43	---	---
New Productions to Date	20	22	---	---
ROAD				
Shows Reported Last Week	24	26	23	28
Total Playing Weeks to Date	593	587	407	319
Total Receipts Last Week	$4,027,459	$3,544,292	$1,213,186	$990,200
Season Total Receipts to Date	$92,795,645	$79,504,943	$22,959,494	$13,606,600
COMBINED TOTALS				
Total Playing Weeks	1,282	1,272	830	724
Total Receipts	$177,466,089	$139,013,148	$44,264,521	$28,999,300

Season box office totals from *Variety.*

product is the production—a play or musical. But, unlike the product in most businesses, the one in the theater, when successful, has magic. People work together for years, using their expertise and talent, to create the magic that will appear on stage. At last the curtain rises on opening night, drawing the audience into the fantasy and excitement of a production it has taken so long to put together.

This is a book about how it all happens. It is about the creation of Broadway's unique product, the people who make the ideas a reality, and the business of putting on plays and musicals.

82   **LEGITIMATE**   Wednesday, November 19, 1980

B'way Up Again; Holiday Helps; 'Lunch Hour,' 'Philadelphia' Strong

Business on Broadway improved again last week, apparently spurred by Veterans Day trade. Total boxoffice receipts rose 7.14%, while paid attendance gained 3.15 points to 77.6% of seating capacity. That brought the figure for the season so far to 73.88%.

Last week's two openings, "Lunch Hour" and a revival of "The Philadelphia Story," received mixed notices but both showed initial b.o. power This week's new entries are "A Lesson From Aloes," which premiered Monday night (17) to favorable reviews, and "The American Clock," due tomorrow night (Thurs.).

"Perfectly Frank" is continuing previews and as of press deadline yesterday (Tues.), this week's only closing is "The Bacchae."

Estimates for Last Week

All reported boxoffice receipts are net — that is, after subtraction of subscription of discounts and theatre party, credit card and computer ticket commissions. In short, the amount on which theatre and production sharing terms are figured and royalties are based. Parenthetical figures immediately

$155,916) (3/30/80) (Sun.) (265p).
PW, $138,596 (7,704; 88.2%).
LW, $152,199 (8,100; 92.7%).
Chorus Line (M), Shubert ($25-$27.50-$30; 1,472; $250,000) (7/25/76) (2,187p).
PW, $202,913 (10,504; 89.2%).
LW, $216,077 (11,099; 94.3%).
Dancin' (M), Broadhurst ($25-$27.50-$30; 1,148; $213,000) (3/27/78) (Sun.) (1,106p).
PW, $158,160 (7,839; 86.2%) (T).
LW, $162,040 (8,054; 87.7%) (T).
Day in Hollywood, Night In Ukraine (M-MB), Royale ($20-$22.50-$25; 1,058; $160,000) (5/1/80) (228p).
PW, $117,438 (6,283; 74.1%).
LW, $134,426 (7,149; 84.5%).
Deathtrap (P), Music Box ($16-$17.50; 1,010; $114,734) (2/26/78) (Sun.) (1,137p).
PW, $61,566 (5,451; 67.5%).
LW, $64,383 (5,626; 69.6%).
Elephant Man (P), Booth ($21-$22.50; 783; $120,000) (4/19/79) (Sun.) (660p).
PW, $118,210 (6,399; 102.16%).
LW, $112,304 (6,217; 99.2%).
David Bowie, the star, missed last Sunday's matinee (16) because of illness.
Evita (M), Broadway ($23.50-$27.50; 1,759; $269,000) (9/25/79)

Variety, the show business trade publication, prints a breakdown of the box office activity for all Broadway shows. This provides an accurate, public record of the status of all Broadway productions.

Commercial Theater
V. Not-for-Profit Theater

There is an incredible amount of theater in the United States today. Practically every town and community has its own amateur theater group. College and university productions are the rule rather than the exception. In elementary schools throughout the country, social studies are often taught through drama, with small children writing and acting in plays about culture and history. Most high schools, as well, have drama organizations that present revivals or, in some cases, original works.

But New York City is the undisputed theater capital of the nation. On a typical day, it is possible to choose from more than eighty productions, ranging from an experimental work in a garage where the admission fee is a small optional monetary contribution, to a large musical on Broadway where a single seat can cost $35.

Broadway, a main throughfare extending the length of Manhattan, has become synonymous with theater in the United States just as London's West End generally means theater in Great Britain. The Broadway area's theaters are located in midtown Manhattan and symbolize the ambitions and dreams of thousands of young people who, each year, come from all over the country hoping to "make it"—as directors, producers, playwrights, designers, and most frequently as actors.

For actors, working on Broadway means a chance to be successful, perhaps even a star—of suddenly being in that enviably rare position of having work come to them rather than continually going out to seek it. Over 80 percent of the members of Actors' Equity, the actors' union, are unemployed as actors at any given time. There are no sudden discoveries in the theater. The reality is years of hard work, going from one audition to another, appearing at small out-of-town dinner theaters and summer playhouses, and most likely, never being able to support yourself as an actor. Yet the myth of overnight success continues, and there are enough success stories in the theater for people to believe that somewhere, somehow, stardom can come suddenly. Barbra Streisand, playing a small part in the forgettable musical *I Can Get It for You Wholesale*, brought down the house each night and became a star. However, even for her, there had been years of auditions, tryouts, and rejection. For Shirley MacLaine, the dream came true one night when she took over the ailing Carol Haney's role in *The Pajama Game* and suddenly went from being an unknown dancer/understudy to stardom.

Broadway means being part of a group that has historically carried a certain mystique—informality, glamour, a risque image. Even the working hours of Broadway are different from the rest of the world's. Theatrical offices don't open before 10:00 A.M., sometimes later. Lunch is often at 3:00 P.M., with dinner after the evening performance. Theater people go to bed late and are still asleep when most other people are in school or at work.

Broadway means prestige. Although movies and television pay much larger salaries, they don't carry the status and esteem of working on Broadway. When Dustin Hoffman starred in his first Broadway play, *Jimmy Shine*, he earned $150,000 in six months. That's not a paltry sum, but he could have earned over half a million dollars in a film assignment that would have entailed only about eight weeks' shooting time.

Physically the Broadway theater district is located in one of midtown Manhattan's least glamorous and attractive areas, amid a variety of pornographic shows, fast food places, and cheap novelty shops. The office buildings housing theatrical producers, managers, and press agents are mostly old and unkempt, nothing like the gleaming new skyscrapers from which the large movie and television corporations operate. Scenic design shops, property warehouses, and costume shops are often in run-down tenement buildings. The theaters, with few exceptions, are themselves old, once elegant buildings with drafty, inefficient dressing rooms and run-down storage areas behind the ornate and beautifully designed stage and seating areas.

Originally, the Wall Street area in lower Manhattan was the city's prime area, the site of its residential, business, and entertainment establishments. As the city's population grew and public transportation became more efficient, the boundaries of the city expanded northward. By the late nineteenth century, New York's theater district was concentrated on Broadway and Sixth Avenue in the twenties and thirties. Most of the theaters offered an assortment of burlesque, minstrel, and other light musical entertainment. They were attended mainly by the lower classes. The rich, who lived in large homes on lower Fifth Avenue, also attended the theater in this district, but usually to see dramatic imports from Great Britain or revivals of established European plays. Opera, which became very stylish in the nineteenth century, was the only musical entertainment attended by New York society. All other musicals were considered disreputable.

Legitimate theater is technically a term used to describe what are now known as straight plays—drama without song, dance, or music. The term is derived from Great Britain's Theatre Act of 1737, which awarded two theaters, the Drury Lane and Covent Garden, the designation "licensed theatre". These were technically the only theaters in England permitted to present what was called legitimate entertainment—plays (including those of William Shakespeare) that had little or no music or singing and consisted entirely of acting.

By the nineteenth century, legitimate theater became a term used to contrast the so-called quality theater attended by the upper classes from the frowned-upon vaudeville, burlesque, and musical revues. Today, the meaning of legitimate theater has become blurred. It still means straight plays, but has come to include musicals as well. In theatrical directories, producers of both musicals and straight plays are listed as "legitimate producers."

In the United States there are now essentially two kinds of theater: commercial and not for profit. Commercial theater is set up as a business. Producers mount plays, either dramas (straight plays) or musicals, and hope to make a profit. They pay income taxes to the state, federal, and city governments on the profits they make. The theaters in which their productions play pay real estate taxes on the property they occupy.

Not-for-profit theater, on the other hand, does not expect to make money from its productions. It applies to the government for nonprofit status and, if its application is approved, the theater does not have to pay taxes. If, by chance, not-for-profit theater does make a profit on a production, the profits go toward additional productions or the upkeep and maintenance of the theater. The people who work for or financially support not-for-profit theater do not benefit financially from a hit play in the way investors in the commercial theater do.

The established commercial theater is today almost exclusively limited to Broadway and off-Broadway. Theaters in large cities such as Boston, Philadelphia and Los Angeles usually house productions that are trying out prior to a New York Broadway opening or touring companies of shows still playing on Broadway or plays that have just completed a successful run. There are other types of commercial theater that do not have the same prestige and status as the Broadway and off-Broadway theater yet are also set up as profit-making institutions.

Bus and Truck

These are productions that tour small towns and college campuses. They are called "bus and truck" because the cast travels to engagements by bus and the sets and props are transported by truck. The trips are often grueling—a series of one-night stands played in small towns, reminiscent of the traveling road companies of years ago. But, because of Equity requirements, salaries and travel and living conditions are much better. For a starting actor, bus and truck offers good experience and, as an added benefit, a lot of free travel across the country.

Bus and truck productions are booked throughout the nation, for the most part by booking agencies located in New York City. The productions performed are usually revivals of past Broadway successes or touring companies of shows still playing on Broadway. However, the bus and truck companies are not the same as the first-class national touring companies of Broadway productions. Often, they are produced by individuals who have purchased the bus and truck rights from the original producers.

Dinner Theater

This is a relatively recent phenomenon. Located primarily in suburban areas, dinner theaters present mostly musicals and light comedies. The price of admission includes a buffet meal, free parking, and the show.

Dinner theaters range in size from under 150 seats to large 1,000-seat complexes. More than half the dinner theaters throughout the nation come under the jurisdiction of Actors' Equity. This means that actors are guaranteed minimum salaries and working conditions. Some actors consider dinner theater very good beginning experience. Some, however, feel that dinner theater is inevitably a low-quality, strictly for profit enterprise that does an actor more harm than good. These actors believe that dinner theater standards are minimal and that a sloppy acting technique can result from dinner-theater experience. Such diverse opinions stem from the particular dinner theater in which an actor has performed. A large, well-run Equity dinner theater committed to quality entertainment does offer good experience to young actors and directors. A non-Equity theater where performers often have to double as waiters and parking-lot attendants is not conducive to either a happy or productive work experience.

Summer Theater/Stock

There used to be a great distinction between summer theater and summer stock. Summer theaters were usually located in or near resort areas and vacation centers. They often housed Broadway productions during the summer months mainly because in the days before air conditioning, many Broadway theaters closed down during hot weather. Summer theaters were often in converted barns or haylofts, hence such names as Music Barn or Hayloft Theatre.

Stock is technically a theater that produces its own plays—that is, its stock. It does not book attractions produced by others. For instance, the Berkshire Theatre Festival in Stockbridge, Massachusetts—a summer resort area in New England—is a summer stock theater. It produces shows using a company of resident actors and technical and artistic personnel (although different directors and stars do work on individual productions). It does not serve as a facility for entire touring productions or personalities. Summer stock used to be, and still is to a lesser extent, the training ground for young actors and actresses. They would work for little or no pay, doing everything from walk-on parts (if they were lucky) to emptying the trash after a performance.

Today, however, with not-for-profit resident theaters in ascendance and offering professional, year-round training to many young actors, summer theaters as profit-making institutions have become almost the equivalent of dinner theaters, albeit without the food. Most of the summer theaters today play revivals of well-known musicals and light comedies of the Neil Simon genre. Increasingly, what is called the "star package" is booked. It may feature a film personality like Rock Hudson touring the summer circuit with *Camelot*, a known television personality appearing in a play, or even a nontheatrical personal appearance by a celebrity such as Joel Grey, Tom Jones, or Engelbert Humperdinck. Summer theaters exist to make money and those who own the theaters and produce the attractions must offer shows and stars that have the best chance of making money—hence, the relatively safe revivals and star packages.

The not-for-profit theaters have really revolutionized theater. Prior to World War II, there were very few not-for-profit theaters in the United States, with the exception of community volunteer theaters. After the war, the off-Broadway movement began as theatre people wanted to produce plays that the commercial Broadway theater would not or could not mount. As the commercial theater must make money to survive, it can produce only those plays that producers and theater owners believe have a chance for popular success—if not on Broadway, at least as films or in subsequent touring, summer, dinner theater or amateur productions.

Certain plays are considered too daring or experimental, or for other reasons are believed to be without the widespread potential appeal necessary for Broadway production. Off-Broadway was born so that these plays could be produced. The off-Broadway theater movement paved the way for not-for-profit theater, of which there are, to-day, many types. Off-Broadway has become more established and is now virtually part of the commercial theater sector; off-off-Broadway has taken its place. The quality of off-off-Broadway ranges from awesomely moving and intimate—eliciting an intensity of experience rarely achieved on Broadway—to badly produced and directed showcases in which aspiring actors and actresses attempt to be "seen." Despite its shortcomings, off-off-Broadway has nurtured and developed many of the better plays that have later achieved commercial success on Broadway. And of equal importance, off-off-Broadway exists as an arena for experimentation and innovation that cannot be done in the commercial sector.

Regional Professional Resident Theater

Often called not-for-profit repertory or regional theater, these permanent theater companies, usually producing plays on a seasonal basis, are located throughout the United States. The use of the word "repertory" is really a misnomer. In a repertory company, the same group of actors works together on a number of plays, rotating parts so that an actor may play a small part in one production and the lead in another. The United States has only a few true repertory companies, the best known being the American Shakespeare Festival in Stratford, Connecticut. It presents a summer season of Shakespeare, usually with the same group of actors. Other well-known repertory companies are the Tyrone Guthrie Theatre in Minneapolis and the Acting Company, an offshoot of New York City's Juilliard School, which tours the nation.

Nowadays, these theaters are really permanent producing organizations that almost always operate under Equity rules, using a particular set of Equity requirements called a LORT (League of Resident Theatres) contract. They are, for the most part, funded and subsidized by the federal government (NEA—National Endowment for the Arts) and state and foundation grants and produce either new plays or revivals of plays of quality. Their producers, directors, and other top management personnel are professionals, who often hold degrees from graduate schools of theater. Increasingly, these theaters serve as the spawning grounds for works that will later come to the Broadway or off-Broadway commercial theater.

Many established actors like to appear in resident theater productions. It gives them the opportunity to do the kinds of plays that they might not be able to do on Broadway. Shakespeare is still the most popular playwright regionally, usually represented with at least one production each season. Because these theaters are not for profit and often sell tickets on an annual subscription basis rather than by single admission, they can produce the kind of plays that more commercially minded operations cannot. New playwrights such as Sam Shepard and David Mamet and the more "difficult" works of playwrights such as Edward Albee and Arthur Kopit appear with some regularity at resident theaters.

Volunteer/Community Theater

These are local theater companies in towns and communities throughout the nation. They range from the purely amateur to fairly established companies which often raise money in order to hire professional directors for their productions. The actors and backstage personnel are usually amateurs who work at other jobs during the day and for whom theater is a hobby. One of the earliest volunteer community theaters was founded by Louisa May Alcott, author of *Little Women*. In 1874, she organized the Concord Players in Concord, Massachusetts, an organization that still exists.

Educational Theater

Most colleges and universities sponsor theaters as part of their drama departments. They produce plays both as part of the drama curriculum and for the community at large.

University and Professional Collaborations

In these productions, students of drama work with professional directors, playwrights, and actors hired from outside academia. The professional actors often assume leading roles and drama students play supporting roles. The Yale Repertory Theatre affiliated with Yale University and offering masters and doctorate degrees in all aspects of theatercraft, is among the most prestigious of these. Several of Yale's productions have made the journey to the commercial theater. Among the most recent is Sam Shepard's Pulitzer Prize–winning play *Buried Child.*

Children's Theater

Most medium-size and large cities have theater groups that produce works only for children. They are supported by government and foundation grants and usually use local church or school facilities for their productions. Only a few children's theater companies, such as Albany, New York's Empire State Youth Theatre and Raleigh, North Carolina's Children's Theatre Company, maintain their own theaters.

2

Every Show Needs A Producer: *Pulling It All Together*

Every theatrical production begins with the producer. The commercial producer may be compared to the head of a large manufacturing company. That person is not only responsible for the finished product but must supervise each step of its production, working to ensure a profit for its stockholders.

In an established not-for-profit company, the producer may be called the artistic director; in a school, the chairman of the drama department; in a small community theater, the president of the association of community players. In any case, all productions—musical or dramatic, commercial or not-for-profit—have a person who functions as producer, regardless of title.

The producer is responsible for the entire process of production, from the selection of the work to the closing of the show. He selects the script; chooses the director and such artistic personnel as choreographer, lighting and set designers; hires the general manager and press agent; and oversees the choice of actors and actresses. It is the producer, too, who bears the responsibility for raising money, because without funds there can be no play. Artistically, producers in the noncommercial theater and in the commercial theater have virtually identical responsibilities. It is in the area of business, particularly in the raising of money, that the responsibilities differ.

The producer in not-for-profit theater must raise money from the public sector (government and foundations) and from individuals who are willing to contribute personal funds to assure an ongoing theater company. In the commercial theater, the producer acts much more as an entrepreneur, raising money for a single production from individuals and businesses and hoping to give these investors a profit.

Broadway producers tend to be businessmen who combine a gambler's streak with a real love and respect for theater. Most producers enter the theater for love and care deeply about their plays and those involved in them. But they do want to protect their investments and those of their backers. They would also like to make money. While most shows lose money, every producer is always hoping for another *Fiddler on the Roof, My Fair Lady* or *Annie*, long-running, profitable, and successful shows.

Just as a successful manufacturer knows and understands his business from the bottom up, a good producer should also understand the workings of his business—the theater. Commercial production is very expensive. It often costs over a million dollars to mount a single production. A novice can easily lose everything by producing on Broadway. Many, if not most, producers active in the commercial theater have worked in the past in theatrical positions such as press agent, director, stage manager, or assistant to a successful producer.

Once a producer does decide to produce, the first step is

to obtain a property from which a play can be developed or to select a play. There are several ways in which this is done.

Original Scripts

Producers annually receive hundreds of scripts written by aspiring playwrights. These scripts are submitted by the playwrights themselves or by agents who represent the playwrights. A playwright has a much better chance of getting a play read if it is submitted by an agent. Producers have working relationships with agents who act as middlemen between writer and producer. Agents receive a percentage of any sale or profit that may be made. Most actors, writers, and entertainers have agents. Good agents, just by association, give professional credibility and standing to the people they represent. In addition, agents can promote and protect clients in a way that is usually impossible for clients to do for themselves. Obtaining an agent is one of the real dilemmas for a person starting out in the entertainment business. It is difficult to get an agent unless you have had some prior success or recognition. And it is difficult to get that success without an agent.

Most producers do look at a large percentage of unsolicited scripts or hire others to read them. But the chances of an unknown playwright's getting a work produced on Broadway are practically nil. The costs of mounting a Broadway production are so high that few, if any, producers are willing to take the risk of producing a first play by an unknown. However, like everything in the theater, it can happen.

On October 6, 1977, a play called *The Gin Game* opened on Broadway. It was a first play, written by D. L. Coburn, a resident of Dallas, Texas. *The New York Times*, a newspaper not given to hyperbole, headlined "Gin Game Author Lives a Miracle" and went on to write, "It is an overnight success story that should make mothers weep for joy."

Mr. Coburn wrote *The Gin Game* and, not having an agent, sent the script to a director whom he had met backstage in a Dallas theater. Through a series of incredibly fortuitous events, *The Gin Game* reached Hume Cronyn; he and his wife, Jessica Tandy, are one of the nation's most distinguished acting couples. Cronyn decided that he wanted to appear on Broadway in *The Gin Game* and showed the script to Mike Nichols, a leading stage producer/director. Nichols agreed to direct *The Gin Game*, and he and Hume Cronyn joined with the Shubert Organization, one of Broadway's most active producing organizations, in bringing the show to Broadway's Golden Theatre.

The Gin Game opened to favorable critical notice and Mr. Coburn was, indeed, an overnight success. It had a very successful run, won a Pulitzer Prize, and toured nationally. The production became one of the first dramatic plays to tour the Soviet Union. However, without the "name" backing of Mr. Cronyn and Mike Nichols, it is unlikely that a new playwright, even of Mr. Coburn's talent, could ever have gotten a first play produced on Broadway.

The more common route to Broadway for a dramatic work by a new playwright is through a loose cooperation that has evolved between not-for-profit regional theaters and off-off-Broadway and the commercial theater. In 1976, a new play, *The Shadow Box*, opened on Broadway and went on to win both the Pulitzer Prize and a Tony Award as best play of the season. *The Shadow Box* had first been produced at the Mark Taper Forum in Los Angeles, one of the nation's most prestigious not-for-profit regional theaters. The Mark Taper is in a position to take the time to work on and develop a new play of merit. A commercially daring play, *The Shadow Box* portrayed three terminally ill characters exploring their feelings and those of their families. It toured nationally and was produced as a special television presentation under the direction of noted actor Paul Newman.

Before the proliferation of not-for-profit theaters throughout the country and before the rising costs of commercial production made artistic risk taking virtually impossible, dramas slated for Broadway played lengthy tryouts in cities throughout the nation. During that period, the playwright, director, and actors often spent weeks rewriting and reorganizing the production. There is an issue, increasingly relevant as government becomes more involved in subsidizing not-for-profit theater, about the propriety of the nonprofit sector serving as a facility for pre-Broadway tryouts. Should the government, however indirectly, subsidize theater to develop plays that then become potential money-makers for those who can afford to invest in the Broadway theater?

An example of this can be seen by following the path of the play *Gemini* to Broadway's Little Theatre, where it opened on May 21, 1977. Albert Innaurato is one of today's outstanding young playwrights. He was a playwright-in-residence at the New York Shakespeare Festival, which, under the direction of Joseph Papp, actually paid playwrights a small weekly salary so that they could afford to practice their craft. His play *Gemini*, a comedic drama about a young man growing up in South Philadelphia, first had a reading at Playwrights Horizons, an off-off-Broadway theater company that often conducts what are called staged readings of works in progress. Innaurato was still working on the *Gemini* script at the time and this informal reading, in front of a small audience, give him the feedback he needed to develop the work further.

Gemini then opened at a not-for-profit community regional theater located in the New York City suburb of Huntington, Long Island—the PAF (Performing Arts Foundation) Playhouse. PAF is a unique facility in that it is both a theater working with the Long Island community and at the same time close enough to New York City to attract the kind of artistic personnel and critical attention from the New York press that other theaters of its status cannot often achieve. *Gemini* played the PAF Playhouse for a limited three-week run. It received favorable critical notices in the New York newspapers, crucial for a play to be successful.

A month later, *Gemini* was presented by the Circle Repertory Company, a prestigious, not-for-profit off-Broadway theater, located in New York City. The play had another successful but limited engagement. At its completion, the Circle Repertory Company joined with the PAF Playhouse and together these two companies brought *Gemini* to Broadway.

One of the longest journeys made to Broadway by a show can be seen by following the route of *Strider*. Robert Kalfin is the producing director of the not-for-profit Chelsea Theater Center, one of New York City's resident theater companies. In 1977, he journeyed to the Soviet Union on a cultural exchange program. While in Leningrad, he saw a play based on a short story by Leo Tolstoy titled "Kholstomer" at the Gorky Theatre, where it is part of the repertory. He felt it would be an ideal production for Chelsea.

The Chelsea Theater Center was able to secure the rights to produce the play in the United States. Kalfin and his collaborators translated the work into English and adapted it to the American stage. It opened at the end of May 1979 as the last production of the Chelsea's 1978–79 season. Called *Strider: The Story of a Horse*, the production received extraordinary reviews.

As a result of these reviews, many people active in the theater went to see *Strider*, including a commercial Broadway producer, Arthur Whitelaw, who had previously developed and produced *You're a Good Man Charlie Brown*. He loved *Strider* and decided to subsidize it through the summer. By advertising and promoting the show, Whitelaw hoped to build a wide audience and move *Strider* to Broadway. *Strider* ran at the Chelsea Theater through the summer and in November moved to Broadway's Helen Hayes Theatre, where it again received highly favorable reviews.

Such a producer, of whom there are increasing numbers, might be called a merchandising producer. Unlike producers who use unproduced scripts obtained from the playwrights themselves or develop productions from primary source material or ideas, a merchandising producer takes a show that has been produced in a not-for-profit or off-off-Broadway setting, nurtures that show through further development and refinement, raises the funds to promote and advertise the show, and then takes the show to the commercial theater. Many merchandising producers used to, and still do, produce plays in the United States that were first successful in Great Britain. However, off-off-Broadway and not-for-profit regional theaters have expanded the available pool of material. These theaters have also created new and vitally necessary outlets for young playwrights and directors.

Books or Existing Scripts

Many producers use books or previously written plays as sources for production ideas. This is particularly true for musicals, the ideas for which are usually conceived by the producer and developed under his auspices.

A producer often buys an option on a book or play script. This is called optioning a property. It gives the producer the exclusive theatrical rights to a story or theme, ensuring that the work will not be developed as a play by anyone else. The producer holds the option for an agreed-upon period of time. If the play is not produced in that time, the option lapses and ownership of the rights reverts back to the author or to whomever the holding producer purchased them from. It is not uncommon for a producer to hold options on many properties at once, sometimes developing only one or none.

If the producer proceeds with the optioned work, he usually hires a playwright (sometimes the original author) to adapt the book into whatever play—musical or straight—he envisions. The play *Golda* is an interesting example. Each step taken toward production was carefully planned, not only to obtain the raw material necessary for development but to generate attention to the upcoming production in order to help raise money and ensure a large advance ticket sale.

In 1975, Golda Meir, the former prime minister of Israel, published her autobiography, *My Life*. The Theatre Guild, one of the oldest producing organizations in the United States, purchased the rights to Mrs. Meir's book. Armina

Marshall and Philip Langner, the mother and son who now head the Theatre Guild, believed that the story of Golda Meir had all the makings of a successful play.

At the same time that the Theatre Guild was negotiating to buy the rights to Mrs. Meir's autobiography, it was making overtures to the distinguished playwright and author William Gibson. The Theatre Guild wanted Mr. Gibson to adapt *My Life* for the stage. They hoped he would create a play that would be not only a drama of Mrs. Meir's life but a drama about Israel and the creation of a nation. The reasons for choosing Mr. Gibson were twofold: he is an outstanding writer and playwright and he is a good friend and colleague of the actress Anne Bancroft.

The Theatre Guild hoped to sign Miss Bancroft to star in the play. Anne Bancroft had made her Broadway debut in Gibson's play *Two for the Seesaw* and starred in *The Miracle Worker*, his play based upon the life of Helen Keller. *The Miracle Worker* had been directed by Arthur Penn, a leading stage and film director. The Theatre Guild believed that Miss Bancroft would want to work on another William Gibson play and also hoped to obtain Arthur Penn to direct. The combination of Gibson, the writer; Bancroft, the actress; and Penn, the director, would, the Theatre Guild felt, make for a successful production, both artistically and financially.

When the Theatre Guild did obtain the rights to *My Life*, even before Messrs. Gibson and Penn and Miss Bancroft were signed for the production, Philip Langner flew to Israel in order to announce the purchase at a press conference with Golda Meir. This event generated a lot of publicity, much more than if a brief announcement had been issued to the press from the Theatre Guild offices. This press attention aided the producers in raising the money necessary to get the production off the ground. A year later, when the play, now titled *Golda*, had been written, Miss Bancroft was flown to Israel for a well-publicized visit with Golda Meir. This increased the advance ticket sale. And when *Golda* opened in New York, the show was already practically sold out for the first four months. It was not, however, a critical success and closed within six months.

It is even more common for musicals to be developed in this manner. *My Fair Lady* was based upon George Bernard Shaw's play *Pygmalion*, and *Fiddler on the Roof* upon some short stories written by Sholom Aleichem. The legendary musical *Oklahoma!* was developed from a play by Lynn Riggs, *Green Grow the Lilacs*, which had been produced by the Theatre Guild in the early 1930s. The Theatre Guild approached the newly formed partnership of Richard Rodgers and Oscar Hammerstein II with the idea for a musical based upon Ms. Riggs's script. *Oklahoma!* began its New York performances on March 31, 1943, having cost its backers $80,000. When it closed after 2,020 performances on May 29, 1948, the show had grossed over $7 million, and was the first show ever to have a cast recording (now an almost routine event for even an unsuccessful musical).

Ideas

Recently, and particularly with musicals, shows have been developed around an idea or concept. Different from the traditional musicals in which a specific plot or story line is based upon a previous straight play or book, these works are generated from a vision in the mind of their creators.

A Chorus Line, the hit musical of the late seventies and early eighties, is the most successful and innovative example of this. Conceived, directed, and choreographed by

The cast from *A Chorus Line*. This opened on Broadway in 1976 and went on to win 8 Tony Awards. One of the theater's blockbuster hits, the production was developed in workshop at the not-for-profit New York Shakespeare Festival, one of the nation's most innovative and best known producing organizations under the leadership of Joseph Papp.

Photo by Martha Swope

Michael Bennett, himself a former chorus dancer, *A Chorus Line* is a tribute to the Broadway gypsies, the term used for the dancers who appear in Broadway musicals. All the elements—dance, music, and dialogue—contribute equally toward developing and exhibiting the idea/concept, the life of a Broadway gypsy. Based on the personal stories of these dancers, *A Chorus Line* is the story of the hopes, hardship, disappointment, and success of those who appear on stage in musical after musical, hoping for a featured (speaking) role and a chance for individual recognition.

Dancin', a hit show of the late seventies and early eighties, was produced by, among others, Bob Fosse, a choreographer/director who is responsible, in a nonproducing capacity, for the success of such shows as *Pippin*, *The Pajama Game*, *Damn Yankees*, *Chicago*, *Cabaret*, and the movie *All That Jazz*. He decided to produce an all-dance musical that hopefully would work as a theatrical piece and not merely a selection of dances performed on the Broadway stage. As an idea, the production was not entirely successful in its execution. Yet, it was a hit, providing audiences an exciting and entertaining evening in the theater.

Other recent idea shows are *Runaways*, developed by Elizabeth Swados along with a group of young actors (some of them actually runaways and based upon their personal stories), and Ntozake Shange's *For Colored Girls Who Have Considered Suicide When the Rainbow Is Enuf*. This show is a moving selection of dance, music, and spoken word which explores the experience of being black women.

What is noteworthy about these idea theater pieces is that they are, almost without exception, developed in workshops by not-for-profit theater companies, often the New York Shakespeare Festival under the sponsorship of Joseph Papp. These shows must be nurtured and developed. They are not traditional theater works for which actors are cast and then rehearse for four to six weeks using a set script, dance steps, and musical numbers. Rather they are developed, formed, and set as they are rehearsed. All components—actors, writer, director, choreographer, lyricist—work together, all contributing skills and insights.

A show that took a middle route, its seeds in a not-for-profit workshop and yet its development strictly for Broadway, was *Grease*, which established a record as Broadway's longest-running musical. Produced by a husband and wife team, Kenneth Waissman and Maxine Fox, *Grease* was not only one of the most financially successful theatrical ventures in history but marked the start for some of the entertainment business's hottest young stars, including John Travolta, Doody in the first Broadway cast and star of *Saturday Night Fever* and the film version of *Grease*; Richard Gere, now a well-known film star; Adrienne Barbeau, Carol in the popular television series "Maude"; Treat Williams, star of the film *Hair*; and Jeff Conaway, star of the television series *Taxi*.

Grease was first presented in Chicago in a theater workshop at the Kingston Mines Theater. The Waissmans journeyed to Chicago to see it after Ken Waissman was urged to do so by a college friend. Immediately, they recognized that they had a possible success and decided to develop the show for Broadway.

They hired choreographer Pat Birch and a relatively unknown director named Tom Moore, whose work they both respected. On February 14, 1972, *Grease* opened at the off-Broadway Eden Theatre (now known as the Entermedia Theatre, on Second Avenue and 12th Street) for a pre-Broadway tryout. The Waissmans purposely picked the Eden because its stage is similar in size and form to many Broadway stages and they wanted to be able to move their production intact to Broadway without having to spend money on rebuilding sets. The show received mixed reviews but audiences flocked to see it, enchanted by the 1950s nostalgia. It moved in June 1972 to the Broadhurst Theatre, and on November 27 of the same year to the Royale, where it established a long-run record.

Stars

Sometimes the availability of a well-known, popular celebrity determines the choice of a play for Broadway. Certain classics come to Broadway because a "name" performer wishes to headline the production. Jason Robards, Jr., is a leading interpreter of Eugene O'Neill. His appearances in *A Moon for the Misbegotten* and *A Touch of the Poet* have been responsible for those successful productions. Paul Scofield's *King Lear* and Richard Burton's *Hamlet* were sell-out Broadway shows, brought to the boards because of the promised commercial success that these two actors could assure.

A name star can often guarantee a successful run, even if the show is a failure. *In Praise of Love* opened at the Morosco Theatre in 1974. Written by the successful playwright Terence Rattigan, the show starred Rex Harrison and Julie Harris. *In Praise of Love*, however, was not up to Mr. Rattigan's usual playwrighting standards and did not receive very favorable reviews. It did, however, have a respectable run and returned a profit to its investors. Without the presence of Rex Harrison and Julie Harris, two actors whom the theater-going public will pay to see even in a mediocre work, *In Praise of Love* would probably have closed fairly soon after its opening.

Most actors and actresses want to appear on Broadway. Not only does a Broadway appearance carry prestige that no movie or television show can match, even more important, a live theater performance gives actors the opportunity to rehearse and develop a role—to practice the craft of acting—which is impossible in any other medium.

Most of the time, however, a well-known celebrity is unwilling to commit himself to a lengthy project requiring the physical and mental stamina necessary for eight performances a week. Often a star joins a show under a contract specifying a commitment for only a limited time. When Richard Burton joined *Equus*, he did so under a six-month contract. When Al Pacino appeared on Broadway in *Richard III*, the play itself was produced for a limited run to accommodate Pacino's schedule.

Sometimes a show is built around a star. *The King and I*, one of the Broadway stage's most successful musicals, was written and produced because the late Gertrude Lawrence, one of the theater's legendary actresses, approached Richard Rodgers and Oscar Hammerstein II with the idea for a musical based upon the novel *Anna and the King of Siam*. The musical turned out to be most memorable and Miss Lawrence played the role of Anna until her tragic death from cancer at the age of fifty-four. *The King and I* later became a successful motion picture starring Deborah Kerr.

Creating a show for a star is, however, a rather risky business. When Katherine Hepburn starred in her only musical, *Coco*, a show based upon the life of the French fashion designer Coco Chanel, the production was written for Miss Hepburn and scheduled around her availability and willingness to appear on Broadway.

As is sometimes the problem with a show in which a big star is the focus, a certain power is given to the star. Katherine Hepburn, the perfectionist that she is, was involved in all facets of the production, even attending most of the auditions. She had requested as director Michael Benthall, who had directed her on film and in Shakespeare when she had performed on tour with England's renowned Old Vic Company. However, Benthall was a dramatic and not a musical director and gradually his job was taken over by the choreographer, a young man named Michael Bennett, whose feats with the earlier discussed *A Chorus Line* were yet to come. The transition was not entirely peaceful. Bennett and Hepburn frequently disagreed over the staging and direction.

Needless to say, Katherine Hepburn's name sold out the show despite the fact that *Coco* itself did not receive very good notices. When she left the Broadway company and another actress took over her role, the box office sales fell drastically and the show closed. However, in order to pay back the investors the more than $900,000 it had taken to bring *Coco* to Broadway, Katherine Hepburn offered to take a salary cut and worked for minimum. She took the production on a national tour until the investors recouped their investments.

More recently, another big star ran into troubles in a Broadway show. A musical entitled *The Act* was created by John Kander and Fred Ebb for Liza Minnelli. Although she won a Tony Award for her performance, it was not a successful piece of theater but rather a showcase for the awesome talents of Miss Minnelli.

One of the problems was that Miss Minnelli was given her choice of director and she chose Martin Scorsese, a highly respected film director but someone who had no previous musical theater experience. The show ran into trouble. Finally Gower Champion was called in to doctor *The Act* while it was in tryout in Chicago. One of the theater's most prominent director/choreographers, Champion was not given directorial credit (he said he wouldn't have accepted it anyway). When *The Act* finally opened on Broadway, it didn't receive good notices and it is most likely that without Liza Minnelli the production would have closed rather quickly.

Champion meanwhile decided to take a hiatus from

the theater, returning in 1980 to choreograph and direct a multimillion-dollar musical, *42nd Street*. Produced by David Merrick, one of Broadway's most flamboyant and successful producers, *42nd Street* marked Merrick's return to Broadway after a sojourn in Hollywood, producing films. Merrick's foibles regarding the press, which are legendary throughout the theatrical community, were once more at work. He canceled a preview performance when he discovered a journalist in the audience. He kept setting and then canceling opening dates. There were rumors about tension between Merrick and Champion. Such talk is not uncommon before openings. It was noted, however, that Champion was not at the theater on occasion and had missed some rehearsals.

42nd Street opened in the late summer of 1980, an obvious success and a personal triumph for Merrick and Champion. After the curtain calls, however, Merrick appeared on stage to announce to the cast, audience, and press Gower Champion's death that afternoon. He had become fatally ill during *42nd Street*'s Washington, D.C., tryouts but continued to work, admitting only to a lingering virus.

Revivals

In the last few years, there have been an increasing number of musicals revived on Broadway—*My Fair Lady, Fiddler on the Roof, Guys and Dolls, Man of La Mancha, The King and I, Hello Dolly, West Side Story,* and *Oklahoma!,* to name a few.

Producers mount revivals for several reasons. Certain musicals and plays have become classics, worthy of being seen by succeeding generations of audiences. In addition, a revival is sometimes less financially risky to produce than a new show. Although musical revivals are expensive, producers feel that there are often better odds for success with a prior hit than with a new production.

For example, *Fiddler on the Roof* returned for a limited run with the late Zero Mostel, who starred in the first production. The combination of *Fiddler on the Roof*, one of the most successful musicals of all time, and Zero Mostel, whose name had become synonymous with the Tevya role, was a sure success.

Guys and Dolls is another example. This successful musical from the early fifties returned to Broadway with a black cast. Its success was due both to the show itself and to the timeliness of presenting a black production—black theatergoers now make up an increasingly large proportion of Broadway audiences.

Increasingly with revivals, there is a national tour before the Broadway engagement. Recent revivals of *Peter Pan*, *Oklahoma!*, and *My Fair Lady*, starring Rex Harrison, toured the United States before opening in New York. Producers know that these shows have a good chance to pay back their production costs while out of town. These tours are both a way of bringing first-class, star-studded revivals to people throughout the nation and also a means of avoiding the risk of opening first on Broadway and receiving negative reviews, which can doom a production.

3

Raising Money for the Show: Angels and Investors

Like any new product, a Broadway show requires money for production. Just like the businessman who decides to manufacture a new toothpaste or beverage, the producer of a show must have a certain amount of money at his disposal with which to develop his product. He also needs funds to sell the show to the public. If the production is a success, he will not only recoup his initial investment, but also make a profit.

The actual raising of money—capitalization, it is called—has become increasingly difficult as the costs of mounting both straight plays and musicals have risen phenomenally over the years. Steadily rising costs are directly responsible for many of the significant changes in the nature of the commercial theater since the beginning of the century. Fewer new plays are presented each season. Those that are, are usually products of off-off-Broadway and regional theater. There are also fewer first-time producers on the Broadway scene each year. Those producers who do produce on Broadway very rarely finance productions out of their own pockets. The costs are simply too great. The few individuals who do have access to the astronomical funds required are not willing to undertake the financial risks entirely on their own.

The 1927–28 Broadway season was the season in which the greatest number of Broadway productions was ever staged: 264 plays opened. The average cost of production was about $10,000 per play. During the 1977–78 season, forty-two new productions opened; during the 1978–79 season, fifty new productions were staged. The average straight play now costs about $300,000 to $500,000 and the average musical between $750,000 and a million dollars. Obviously, the stakes are high. The saga of one musical, *Got to Go Disco*, is typical of what can happen on Broadway.

A new musical created to capitalize on the national disco dancing craze, *Got to Go Disco* opened in May 1979 at the Minskoff Theatre, one of Broadway's largest musical theaters, seating 1,621 people. The most expensive production ever to open on Broadway, "Got to Go Disco" cost more than $2 million to produce (some estimates go as high as $5 million). It received resoundingly bad reviews and closed after one week. To make matters worse, the theater interior had to be practically completely rebuilt to accommodate the elaborate sets and sound system. When the show closed, the producer received a bill for $100,000 from the Minskoff, the cost of restoring the theater to its prior state.

The following season, however, a new record was established with the most expensive one night stand in history. *Frankenstein*, a play about a man-made monster based on the story by Mary Shelley, opened on January 4, 1981 and closed the same night after receiving almost unanimously poor reviews.

With an original budget of $500,000, the saga of its production paralleled its own plot. It had become a monster out of control. By the time *Frankenstein* opened, it had cost over $2 million and had eaten the cash reserve earmarked for post-opening advertising and promotion. Unusually elaborate and mechanically complicated sets, special effects of the type usually confined to high budget science fiction films, a large crew of stagehands, three opening night postponements and inflation contributed to the cost escalation.

And, as if such sums weren't enough of a hurdle, even before the funds needed for the actual production can be solicited or raised, the producer must have money to cover the expenses necessary to getting things started. If the show is to be a musical, the lyricist, composer, and librettist (author) must be paid for their work in developing the show. Sometimes the creative people will work for nothing, knowing that if the show is a hit they will collect substantially. However, this is rare, and the producer must have money available to pay those responsible for actually creating the show.

Even if the show is playing off-off-Broadway or in a regional theater and the producer plans to move it to Broadway, there are expenses to cover. Scripts must be printed. Office expenses such as phone bills and rent must be paid. If there are to be cast replacements, a casting director and audition space are hired. The attorneys retained to work out the many complicated legal details and the financial advisers who prepare the capitalization (production) budget—the specific breakdown of expenses for each aspect of production—must be paid.

The money needed to cover these expenses is called front money. Front money is simply the money required to get the future production to the point where there is a specific project for which to raise the major portion of the funds. The amount of front money required and the subsequent sums necessary to produce the show have made it increasingly common for producers to join together in their efforts. Under a legally binding contract called a joint venture agreement, individuals agree to become partners and work jointly as coproducers. A theatrical program or press release announcing a new production will often reflect this kind of partnership.

Another category of producer is becoming increasingly common as production costs increase—the associate producer. This usually means one thing: money. The listing of an associate producer indicates that that person or organization has been instrumental in raising money for the production. Ordinarily, an associate producer does not participate in the creative decisions or day-to-day operations of a show but only in raising a large enough sum to receive associate producer credit.

The Limited Partnership

The producer does not undertake the complicated and expensive task of raising money until the specifics of the production are final. There is a working script and, if the production is a musical, most of the music and lyrics are completed. Most likely, a director has been selected, as has most of the cast. At this point, a special type of company for production, called a limited partnership, is formed.

Created by a legal document called a limited partnership agreement, this type of company has been developed specifically to protect investors while giving them certain tax benefits. The limited partnership agreement must be approved by the appropriate government agency. Depending upon the actual number of investors and their place of residence, either the New York State attorney general or the federal government's Securities and Exchange Commission must approve the agreement. Only then can the producer actually begin raising money for the production.

A document called an offering circular is prepared. It is designed to tell potential investors everything they would want to know to help them make a decision about whether to invest in the show. It contains a synopsis of the plot; biographies of the producers and key artistic personnel; and a full description of the financial and structural organization of the limited partnership company. Potential investors are informed of the specific date on which their investments will be returned if the producer fails to raise the total amount of money required for the production. This way, no producer can tie up an author's work or an investor's funds indefinitely.

Unique to the theater, because it is such a high-risk investment, a statement about the risks of theatrical investment is included in the offering circular. Following is a typical statement, which is always placed under the heading "The Risk to Investors."

1. The sole business of the Partnership will be the production of the Play as a first-class production on Broadway. In such a venture, the risk of loss is especially high in contrast with the prospects of profit. These securities should not be purchased unless the investor is prepared for the possibility of total loss.

2. While no accurate industry statistics are available, it has been claimed that of the plays produced for the New York stage in the 198__–198__ season, a vast majority resulted in loss to investors.

3. On the basis of presently estimated expenses, the Play would have to run for a minimum of ____ weeks on Broadway to a full capacity house in order to return to the Limited Partners their initial contributions. A vast majority of the plays produced for the New York stage in the 198__–198__ season failed to run this long. Those that did, played to capacity audiences.

4. The General Partner may abandon the production of the play at any time for any reason whatsoever.

There are two categories of partners in a limited partnership: general partners and limited partners. The general partners are the producers in fact. They are the individuals whom the theatergoer associates with the show. They make all the decisions about the day-to-day operation of the production company; hire and fire personnel; choose the theater; approve advertising and promotional materials; decide when the show will open and if and when it will close. As producers, the general partners receive 50 percent of any profits made. In addition, whether or not the show is actually making a profit, they may receive a percentage of the total box office receipts each week and a sum of money toward their office expenses. For a Broadway production, the office reimbursement usually is about $600 a week.

The limited partners are the actual cash investors. They are called limited partners because they are responsible only for the amount of their agreed-upon investment. If, for instance, the show closes immediately after opening and the production company owes money, the limited partners do not have to worry about being sued or assessed any additional sums to pay the company's debts. The general partners, however, are liable. The limited partners share the remaining 50 percent of any profits in proportion to their respective investments. If the show does not make a profit, the limited partners lose their investment. However, they may treat this as a loss for income tax purposes.

Sometimes, the limited partners are responsible for an additional sum of money called an overcall. This is a sum, usually amounting to 10 percent of the initial investment, which may be required before the show is produced. The percentage of any possible overcall is also stated in the offering circular given to potential investors. A commitment to come up with the overcall is part of the agreement made by the limited partner.

If after reading the offering circular potential investors decide to invest, they purchase shares and sign the limited partnership agreement. These shares are called units. Usually, investment in a production company is divided into one hundred units. This is true whether the production is a multimillion-dollar musical or a lower-budget straight play. An investor usually purchases a minimum of one unit block, although sometimes half or even quarter units can be purchased. This is true especially in the case of a high-budget production where even one unit can represent a tremendous sum of money.

Although general partners rarely invest their own funds to finance their productions, they are sometimes forced into it. Sometimes a producer attempting to raise money for a show reaches a point where all the funds are raised except one last remaining chunk. At that point, producers have been known to use their life savings or to refinance their homes. But what happens most often is that the producer gives up a portion of his own 50 percent profit share to obtain what is called the "end" or "last" money. The production is now almost a sure thing. A theater has probably been booked; actors are waiting to start rehearsal; sets are designed and all systems are waiting to go. The producer will often make any deal he must in order to obtain that last bit of money. When a show cannot raise the last needed amount, power is in the hands of the person who comes up with it. A producer can have a hit show and make very little profit because he has had to give away so much of his 50 percent share to obtain the final capitalization.

Edward Albee is one of the nation's leading playwrights. He has won the Pulitzer Prize twice and his play *Who's Afraid of Virginia Woolf?* is one of the theater's most frequently performed works. It was a hit film starring Elizabeth Taylor and Richard Burton. In 1980, when Albee's new play, *The Lady from Dubuque*, was about to go into rehearsal, the production company lost a major investor. The theater had been booked. Paulene Trigere, a famous designer, had begun work on the star's costume. The cast, which included such stellar personalities as Irene Worth, Earle Hyman, and Tony Musante, was gathered in New York ready to begin rehearsals. An opening date had already been set. However, the show couldn't begin rehearsal because the last chunk of money hadn't yet been raised. Each day of rehearsal missed was cause for alarm. The opening couldn't be postponed because Alan Schneider, the director, had a previous commitment outside New York immediately following the show's scheduled opening.

The New York Times publishes a column on Wednesdays and Fridays consisting of news and items about the theater. The producers of *The Lady from Dubuque* quite openly told *The New York Times* about their plight and it was duly published. (The *Times* was willing to print the story. One doesn't tell the *Times* what to print.) The money was finally raised. But what had originally been a production with two producers became a show with six general partners. The two original producers undoubtedly had to give up a substantial amount of their 50 percent share to obtain that last money. Rehearsals began two weeks late. The story, however, did not have a happy ending, for when *The Lady from Dubuque* opened on Broadway, it received almost unanimously negative notices and closed one week after opening.

Money Sources

Most producers have people who have invested in their previous shows. They are called angels or backers. The ease with which a producer can obtain backing often depends upon his track record. A producer who has had a large percentage of hit plays and whose name is connected with success has a much easier time obtaining backers than an unknown or someone with a series of failures.

Producers obtain backers in several ways. They keep lists of all those who have invested in one of their productions. By law, the names of all limited partners in production companies are published in the *New York Law Journal* and at least one other publication that is authorized to print legal notices. Lists of possible backers can be obtained by culling back issues. A publication listing all Broadway angels is put out by the entertainment trade publication *Show Business*. However, this is probably no better as a source than the *Law Journal* because it is merely a compilation of its published lists. A producer may also go through the names of attorneys and physicians and other affluent groups listed in the Yellow Pages in the hopes that some will be interested in a theatrical venture.

Recently, and particularly in the case of musicals which

are so expensive to produce, producers have begun to reach
out to the general public by placing advertisements in
newspapers such as *The New York Times* and the *Wall
Street Journal* in the hopes of attracting potential investors.
A record-breaking 323 investors put money into the ill-fated
musical *I Remember Mama*, which was capitalized at
$1,250,000. Alexander H. Cohen, the producer, had placed
ads in newspapers in Boston, Philadelphia, Washington,
Atlanta, Miami, Detroit, Houston, Dallas, and Seattle, an
unprecedented move in the financing of a Broadway show.
Individual backers put up half the money, Universal Pictures the remainder.

Initially, *I Remember Mama* seemed to have all the
elements for success (if such words can ever be used about a
Broadway show). Its star was the Norwegian actress Liv
Ullman. Her presence alone should have meant business at
the box office. It had one of Broadway's best-known producers, Alexander H. Cohen, who produces the annual nationally televised Tony Awards presentation each spring.
Its composer was the late Richard Rodgers, returning to the
theater after a long hiatus; his music for *Oklahoma!*, *The
King and I*, and *Carousel* to name a few, are now standard
tunes throughout the world. And it had Martin Charnin as
director and lyricist; his lyrics and staging of *Annie* were in
no small way responsible for the blockbuster success of
that show.

The story of *I Remember Mama* had a long and successful history. The writer, Kathryn Forbes, had published
a series of vignettes in the *Reader's Digest* about a large
family of Norwegian immigrants living in San Francisco at
the turn of the century. In 1943, the pieces were published
as a book, entitled *Mama's Bank Account*. In 1944, John

Van Druten dramatized the book for the producing debut of Richard Rodgers and Oscar Hammerstein II, who had so recently made theatrical history with their stunning production of *Oklahoma!*. The play (which incidentally featured an unknown actor named Marlon Brando as the young son, Nils) was a success and was produced as a movie in 1948. In 1949, "I Remember Mama" became a CBS weekly television series which ran for seven years, one of the most popular and successful series ever produced.

When Martin Charnin started to think about reviving the story for Broadway, it seemed timely and sound. It was a warm and human story, reflecting the ideal of the family in a time when the whole structure of traditional family life seemed to be in question. And, *Mama*'s potential audience was probably the very same people who had watched "I Remember Mama" on television, now grown-up theatergoers.

However, *I Remember Mama* turned into one of those theatrical nightmares that everyone dreads. The production went to Philadelphia for a pre-Broadway run. It opened to uniformly bad reviews, after postponing its opening for several weeks. Alexander Cohen relieved Charnin, first as director and then as lyricist, at which point Charnin sent telegrams to the New York, Los Angeles, and Detroit companies of *Annie* saying: "Ms. Ullman and I do not see 'I to I' about how musicals are made. To make a long and ugly story short, there's no longer a fjord in my future." Charnin went on to suffer a heart attack from which, fortunately, he recovered fully; it is likely that it was, in part, caused by the stress of his whole experience with *Mama*. When *I Remember Mama* did open in New York in the spring of 1979, it opened to mixed reviews and closed after a three-month run.

Backers' Auditions

One of the traditional ways in which money is raised for Broadway production is through backers' auditions. These are a throwback to the times when producers maintained active offices, producing year after year and often several plays at once. Many of these producers had regular backers who routinely invested in their shows. As a courtesy, the investors were invited to previews of the new shows. These backers' auditions were designed to keep the backers happy and involved by making them part of the glamour of the theater and the lure of Broadway.

Today, backers' auditions are held in large, attractive apartments or in a restaurant (Sardi's, the theater district's most famous eating place, is a common spot). Producers invite potential investors for cocktails. If a star has already been lined up for the production, the producers make every effort to have the star present, to add to the glamour of the situation. The producers then proceed to explain their plans for the show and give a brief description of the plot. They display sketches of costumes and sets. A few of the songs are sung to a piano accompaniment and questions asked by potential investors are answered. Following the audition, there is some socializing and the investors are given a copy of the offering circular and limited partnership agreement to read.

Backers' auditions are fun. People love to feel wanted and they are pleased to be courted by important theatrical figures in such an agreeable situation. However, backers usually decide to invest in a show because of the creative people involved and the facts presented in the offering circular and not as a direct result of attending a backers' audition. For the reality is that it is difficult to get a real sense of what the production will actually be like. By the time the show opens, it will have undergone substantial changes. It is impossible to see what works until the material and actors are on stage. Because this is so, it is entirely possible that the show that backers see on opening night bears little resemblance to the production in which they thought they were investing.

Corporate Investors

Because Broadway production involves so much money, especially in the case of musicals, individual investors can rarely even collectively come up with enough money to finance a show. So, in addition to the individual angels who invest, large corporations often come in as backers. If the show is a hit, the corporations make huge profits, just as individual investors do.

For instance, in 1956, when *My Fair Lady* was first produced, it was capitalized at $400,000. CBS financed the entire production, ultimately making more than $42 million back on its initial investment. More recently, Annie received $100,000 of its $800,000 capitalization from Columbia Pictures. As of September 1979, Columbia had received $256,000 beyond this initial investment, a profit of over 150 percent.

It is logical for entertainment enterprises to invest in Broadway shows. Doing so allows them to reap benefits far beyond simple investment profits. Often, as a condition of its investment, a record or motion picture company will receive the first rights to bid on a cast recording or motion picture. Or it will receive the right to cast the final bid, offering as little as a dollar more than the highest bid, thus assuring for itself the huge potential profits to be derived from recording or movie rights. Here's how it works. *Annie* was sold to Columbia Pictures for $9.5 million—the largest movie sale ever of a Broadway show. As an investor in the production, Columbia was in a position to acquire those rights. In another case, CBS, which is both a television network and a recording company, obtained as a condition of its investment in *My Fair Lady* the first rights to make the cast recording of that show. The record turned out to be one of the best-selling recordings ever made, and CBS made profits both as an investor in the show and as producer of the cast recording.

However, such profits are the exception. In 1978, a show called *Platinum* opened on Broadway. Capitalized at $1.25 million, the show had its genesis, as do many shows that come to Broadway, in a regional theater, Buffalo's Studio Arena. At that time, the show was called *Sunset*. Basically a love story between a 1940s film star trying to make a comeback as a recording artist and a young rock idol, *Sunset* had all the attributes for success: Alexis Smith, a Tony Award–winning actress with tremendous box-office appeal, as star; a recording studio setting with contemporary disco/music and dancing; and a love story. In other words, it had potential box office appeal to both young and older audiences.

Paramount Pictures became interested in the production. Its executives traveled to Buffalo to see the show. They decided to invest $300,000 and, in return, got the opportunity to cast the final bid for a movie sale. Paramount was not just investing in the show. The possible loss of $300,000 is not unusual for such a company. It was investing in the possibility that *Sunset* might turn into a hit. They would then move to obtain the film rights to produce the film. But the show, which opened under the name *Platinum*, received negative reviews and closed quickly.

Producers are obviously anxious for the backing of large

corporations. Not only does a corporate investment provide a substantial amount of money, it provides credibility and status to the planned production. Individual investors become more interested in purchasing units when they hear that a major business concern believes enough in the show to put up funds. Increasingly, movie and television companies retain advisers on staff whose job it is to look for possible Broadway properties in which to invest. It is not unheard of for one such company to be the sole investor in a Broadway show.

Universal Pictures financed and produced the hit show *The Best Little Whorehouse in Texas*. They developed the production at off-Broadway's Entermedia Theatre (in the same way that *Grease* producers Ken and Maxine Waissman did), with the intention of moving the production to Broadway. When *The Best Little Whorehouse in Texas* did move, it became a hit, spawning a first-class national touring company starring Alexis Smith and a film to be released in 1981 with Burt Reynolds and Dolly Parton.

4

The Business of Theater: Budgets, Contracts, Egos, Unions, etc.

The General Manager

When producers feel fairly certain that they have found or developed a property, they begin to work with a general manager. This happens even before they can start to raise money for the show. It is part of the job of the general manager to prepare the materials that will be included in the offering circular and limited partnership agreement.

Theoretically, the progression of a Broadway show from inception to stage can be plotted in chronological order. But it rarely works that way in fact. One of the real dilemmas in commercial production is that a producer must proceed as if he is sure the show will come together. He must arrange for set and costume designers to start work, pay front money to lawyers and lease money for the theater, and engage stars and other cast members. And he can only hope that all of the many elements will come together at the right time to allow production to begin on time.

All theatrical organizations have someone who functions as a general manager. In a not-for-profit theater, the title may be "managing director." The general manager acts as the producer's surrogate. On behalf of the producer, he oversees all of the nonartistic parts of theatrical production. The general manager must combine many skills. He must be a good negotiator. Under instruction from the producer, he will often be the one to work directly with the agents or lawyers of actors and other artistic people in drawing up contracts. He may also have to negotiate the lease for the theater. He must be knowledgeable about accounting and financial procedures as his office will handle funds and draw up budgets. Also, the general manager must have a thorough understanding of the various theatrical union rules because the Broadway theater is among the most unionized businesses in the nation. Most general managers have a theatrical background, having themselves worked as stage managers, company managers, or even actors.

In the United States, the current general manager role evolved from the nineteenth century actor/manager, director/manager, or playwright/manager. As the terms imply, these were impresarios who formed their own dramatic companies, similar to resident stock organizations today. The companies were formed primarily to showcase the talents of the founder, be it as a director, playwright, or actor.

Housed in their own theaters, these actor or director or playwright/managers produced a season of theatrical presentations, engaging an ensemble of actors and other theatrical personnel, including set designers, propertymen, and carpenters, all of whom worked on each production. As is true today, stars were frequently brought in to act in individual productions; but basically the theatrical organization—artistic and nonartistic—remained as a working company under the direction of one individual. Among the best known of these were David Belasco and Edwin Booth, both of whom have legitimate theaters named for them.

David Belasco was one of the most flamboyant and idiosyncratic American stage personalities. He was totally immersed in the fantasy of the theater. He usually wore the clerical collar of a priest. At one point, he was so successful that he had two performing theaters in New York. One, the Belasco, located on 44th Street, was built with a ten-room duplex apartment on top in which Belasco lived. Still in existence today as a Broadway house, the Belasco is said to be haunted by its namesake, who has been sighted on occasion by stagehands and actors.

A playwright as well as manager, Belasco's melodramas *Madame Butterfly* and *The Girl of the Golden West* provided the basis for Puccini's popular operas of the same names. However, Belasco's plays are remembered more for their flamboyance than enduring quality. His greatest contributions to the theater were his pioneering advances in stage settings and lightings. Belasco once created an exact replica of Child's Restaurant, a famous Broadway area eating place. He did this for his 1912 production of a play called *The Governor's Lady*. The setting was accurate down to the last cup and saucer. When Belasco built the theater that now bears his name, he installed the most advanced lighting system of the day, including the first concealed footlights on an American stage.

Edwin Booth, a member of one of the most distinguished theatrical families of all time, was best known for his performances in Shakespeare's tragedies. His 1864 production of *Hamlet* ran for a hundred performances. These days, one hundred performances is not significant but then it was a record breaker. Booth's theater, specially built for him on 23d Street, was the first theater to be constructed with specially powered elevators under the stage to raise and

lower scenery. An artistic success but a financial disaster, the theater forced Booth into bankruptcy within five years of construction because it was so expensive to operate.

Booth was the son of English actor Junius Brutus Booth, who immigrated to the United States. Edwin Booth's two brothers were actors as well. The entire Booth family appeared once together on stage in a production of *Julius Caesar* at Booth's first theater, the Metropolitan. The production is today of historical importance for another reason as well. It marked the last stage appearance of Edwin Booth's brother, John Wilkes Booth, before he went on to gain notoriety as the assassin of Abraham Lincoln in Washington's Ford Theatre. John Wilkes Booth is said to have left a "line of evil" across the stage as he crossed it, attempting to escape from the scene of the assassination. Actors who have played Ford's say that they can sometimes feel a drop in temperature as they cross this line.

Edwin Booth's home on Gramercy Park is now the site of the Players, a private theatrical club, whose library is one of the best sources of theatrical information. It houses one of the most impressive collections of memorabilia in the nation.

The nineteenth-century resident stock company system functioned quite well. It was fairly economical, for with a certain amount of planning, sets could be recycled or refurbished for several shows. It also provided somewhat steady employment to groups of actors. However, as the nation grew and the railroad system was developed and expanded,

Edwin Booth, one of the 19th Century's foremost interpreters of the works of Shakespeare (and the brother of John Wilkes Booth, Abraham Lincoln's assassin) in the role of *Hamlet.*

Photo courtesy of Culver Pictures

suddenly it became possible to bring entertainment to the hinterlands. Not only was this feasible, it was potentially highly profitable. Around the turn of the century, there were approximately five thousand theaters in cities of varying sizes throughout the nation. With no television, film, or radio, only live entertainment was available to people. They wanted it and were willing to pay for it.

This period heralded the beginning of the producer's role as we know it today. A manager/producer would book a show into a New York theater. If the show was a success, he would organize road companies much like today's bus and truck to travel throughout the nation presenting the show "direct from New York." Not only did this new trend call for a more organized and tighter management, the business details suddenly assumed new importance. Good management meant more profit. This started a trend that has continued up to today.

It is almost mandatory for the business and artistic aspects of the theater to have separate overseers. Today, the sheer expense and complexity of production has made it imperative that there be a person to represent the producer in overseeing management and costs. Artistic responsibilities are different from management responsibilities. Artistic people—actors, director, playwright, designers—have a responsibility to translate their ideas into the highest-quality professional production possible. The producer has an obligation to protect the investors, insofar as anyone can protect theatrical investors, and ensure that their money is used responsibly. Someone must monitor financial decisions and attempt to manage as efficiently as possible what is unavoidably, an unwieldy organization.

Today, general managers on and off-Broadway work in

several ways. Some maintain their own offices, handling the shows of many producers simultaneously. Others work full time for the few producing organizations that maintain continuously operating offices. General managers employ company managers. Company managers are members of a theatrical union, the Association of Theatrical Press Agents and Managers (ATPAM). Their job is to handle the business and financial affairs of one show at a time. Company managers usually work in the general manager's office during the day, but must be at the theater for each performance. The company manager corroborates and signs the box office statement for each performance. This is an accounting of ticket sales showing profit and loss. It is given to the producer and is available to all those receiving shares of the total box office receipts.

Budgets

Preparing a budget is a very complicated task and it is here that the theatrical background of a general manager becomes particularly important. Preparing a budget is not simply a matter of drawing up a list of itemized expenses under appropriate headings. The budget must reflect, as accurately as possible, the final form the production will take. And it is during the budget preparation process that much of the actual production is defined.

The budget evolves by answering questions. For instance, most general managers and producers consult the playwright and the director to get a sense of what kind of production they envision. What kind of set will there be? Will it be large and complicated to construct, involving moving scenes and specially built equipment? Or will it be a simple set, remaining in one place on stage? Will there be visual effects such as film clips or slides? What kind of lighting is anticipated? Will the costumes be elaborate period pieces requiring extensive handwork? Will they be purchased in a department store or will they be rented from a costume supply house? Will a famous (and expensive) designer be asked to do the costumes? Is there going to be music? If so, how big an ensemble? How much salary and what percentage of the box office receipts will the star receive? What extras are required? (For instance, when Yul Brynner starred in the recent revival of *The King and I*, he was provided with a limousine and chauffeur to take him to and from the theater for each performance, and his dressing room was totally refurbished.) Will a television commercial be filmed before the opening? Is the show going to have a pre-Broadway tryout outside New York or will it go directly into its New York theater?

The answers to these questions, and many more, are incorporated into the budget. And, since it is at this point that the projected form and scope of the production really begin to take shape, the preparation of the budget becomes not only a financial breakdown of the production but also one of the key steps during which the show begins to take on life.

The general manager prepares two budgets: the capitalization or production budget and the operating budget. The production budget is the amount of money required to open the show and is the sum the producer must raise from investors. The operating budget is the sum required to run the show each week after it has opened. The figure at which a show breaks even is called the "nut," any revenue after that being profit. This term is derived from medieval times, when troupes of players went from town to town, often traveling in a wagon that could be converted into a stage. Most towns and villages required the payment of a tax or fee. To make sure the troupe didn't leave before paying the tax, town authorities often removed a nut from one of the wheels so that the wagon could not be moved. When the tax was paid, the nut was put back in place and the troupe could move on. Recouping the nut is the term used when a show meets its weekly operating expenses.

Both budgets, production and operating, are part of the offering circular given to potential investors. A typical production budget appears below. This is for a small musical capitalized at $502,405, and represents costs as of fall, 1979. It is almost certain that within six months these figures would have increased substantially, for such is the trend of Broadway production.

Scenery

Designer	$ 5,000
Painting & Building	35,000
Assistant	358
Props Build	4,500
Drape Purchase	6,000
Pension and Welfare	589
Set Supervisor	5,000

Costumes

Supervisor	4,000
Assistant	716
Building	10,000
Wigs and Accessories	2,750
Pensions and Welfare	627
Designer	2,750

Lighting and Sound

Designer	3,000
Assistant	1,010
Tape Preparation	5,000
Sound Designer	2,750
Sound Guarantee	8,000
Light Guarantee	8,000
Pension and Welfare	403

Rehearsal

Director	5,000
Cast	17,573
Understudies	3,728
Stage Managers	7,550
Conductor	3,625
Musicians	1,750
Hall	4,000
Scripts	1,000
Stage Manager's Expense	300
Piano	500
Casting/Auditions	3,000
Choreographic Assistant	2,750
Crew	8,975
Rehearsal in Theater	3,250

Transportation and Cartage

Local Transfer (In & Out)	3,000
Director/Author	750
Misc.	1,000

Music

Copying	7,500
Arrangements	2,000
Orchestrations	14,000
Supplies	2,000

Advertising and Publicity

Preliminary Advertising	35,000
Posters & Artwork	6,500
Press Agent	2,875
Press Agent Expenses	1,000
Post Opening Advertising	35,000
Marquee & Front of House	5,000
Photocall and Photos	2,500

Miscellaneous

Office Fee	4,200
Pension and Welfare	3,100
Payroll Taxes	6,500
General Manager	5,000
Acquisition of Rights	2,500
Preliminary Box Office	3,500
General Manager's Rehearsal Fees	7,000
House Preliminaries	1,000
Legal	15,000
Accounting	6,000
Closing Expenses	5,000
ATPAM Pension and Welfare	660
Company Manager's Salary	2,500
Insurance	10,000
Telephone	1,000
Production Secretary	2,500
Group Sales and Mailing	4,000
Miscellaneous	3,000
Opening Night Expenses	750
Contractor	500

Bonds and Recoupables

Author's Advance	4,500
Actors' Equity	23,476
IATSE	3,990
ATPAM	2,650
AFM	10,000
Theater	17,500
Two Weeks of Previews	70,000

Once the budget is prepared, the general manager may become relatively inactive until most of the money has been raised and the show begins production.

Sometimes, however, and increasingly with big budget musicals, where it is known from the outset that a major business is going to finance a good portion of a show, the producer, acting through a general manager, immediately goes on to the second part of the job: negotiating contracts, and dealing with the theatrical unions and professional societies.

Unions

The commercial theater is one of the most unionized businesses in the nation. Almost every job in the theater, whether wardrobe mistress or press agent, comes under the jurisdiction of a union or professional society. These organizations mandate minimum fees or salaries, working conditions, and nearly every other aspect of employment. In mounting a Broadway production, by the time the show actually gets on the stage, contracts have been signed with personnel representing at least twelve trade and professional organizations.

Most minimum basic salaries and fees are negotiated with each union and professional society by the League of New York Theatres and Producers, a body composed or producers and theatre owners. However, individual contracts are signed between producer and/or theatre owner and the individuals they employ. Obviously, not everyone works for minimum and that is where negotiating skills become most important.

Organizations with whom the producer signs contracts are:

1. Dramatists Guild: the professional organization for playwrights and musical composers, authors, and lyricists.
2. Actors' Equity Association: the trade union to which all actors in the legitimate theater belong.
3. United Scenic Artists of America: the union to which all scenic, costume, and lighting designers belong.
4. Wardrobe Supervisors and Dressers: the union to which all costume and wardrobe personnel belong.
5. Society of Stage Directors and Choreographers.

Organizations with whom the theater owner signs contracts are:

1. International Alliance of Theatrical Stage Employees (IATSE): the union to which theatrical carpenters, stagehands, electricians, sound technicians, and property crewmen belong.
2. Treasurers and Ticketsellers Union.
3. Service Employees in Amusement and Cultural Buildings: the union for porters and cleaners.
4. International Union of Operating Engineers: the union to which all heavy equipment maintenance personnel belong.
5. Legitimate Theatre Employees Union: the union for ushers and doormen.

Organizations with whom both the producer and theater owner must sign contracts are:

1. Association of Theatrical Press Agents and Managers (ATPAM): the union to which press agents, company managers, and house managers belong. The producer signs the contracts with the press agent and company manager, the theater with the house manager.

2. American Federation of Musicians: the musicians' union. By contract, certain theaters must employ a minimum number of musicians, even if the production has no music and is a straight play. These union members are called "walkers." They pick up their paychecks and walk away. But if the theater is housing a musical and musicians are actually required for the production, those contracts are signed by the producer.

There are several reasons for the existence of so many unions in the theater, the main one being to protect employees in a business where not only is money lost most of the time, but the show—the business—can cease to exist almost overnight. If one works for the Ford Motor Company and a new car design doesn't sell, the particular car is discontinued but the Ford Motor Company stays in business. Some employees may be laid off, but most of the time those who have worked on the automobile are transferred to another department or immediately given another project. Even if they are laid off and must go on unemployment insurance, employees are usually given severance pay. Ford remains in business and doesn't disappear without paying such things as back wages and vacation pay. In the theater, however, if the show doesn't run, it simply closes. Everyone is out of work. Hopefully, the production company still has funds with which to pay outstanding bills. But this is not always the case.

Unions and professional societies exist to guarantee that their members, the theatrical employees, are paid weekly salaries or agreed-upon fees. They also specify the conditions under which their members work, even, as in the case of Actors' Equity, describing such seemingly minute details as the temperature of the space in which auditions may be held (at least 68 degrees) in a rule book that is over one hundred pages long.

Many of the unions insist that a bond be posted at the time a contract is signed. The bond is usually a sum of money amounting to two weeks' salary. These funds are held by the union in a special account and are released back to the production company only when the union is positive the employees have been paid. If the show closes and the producer runs out of money, the payments due are taken out of the bond held by the union.

A look at Actors' Equity, the largest theatrical union, shows why and how unions became so important in the theater. Actors' Equity was organized in 1913 with the intention of getting producers to sign standard contracts with actors which would provide for minimum pay and minimally satisfactory working conditions. In the early part of the century, actors anxious for work took jobs under arduous, unfair conditions, as some still do today.

Because theater was about the only entertainment available to people, there were literally dozens of small touring companies crisscrossing the nation. The producers didn't have to pay minimum salaries or any health benefits, so they could keep costs fairly low and could start such a traveling troupe with very little capital.

Actors in touring companies were often left stranded in the middle of the country when a producer decided to close the show. It was up to the actor to arrange for transportation home, perhaps from a place as far from New York as Fargo, North Dakota—no easy task in 1900 or 1910, especially in the middle of winter.

To get parts, actors had to rehearse for weeks at a time without pay and a producer could demand that they play extra performances for no extra pay. Actors had to furnish their own costumes out of the small amount of money they were paid. On top of that, they were responsible for the maintenance of their costumes—no small expense, given the wear and tear of travel and performances in theaters with minimal conveniences. An actor who got sick was dependent upon the good will of the producer or traveling manager for medical care. In addition, many actors were forced to sign a "satisfaction clause," which gave the manager or producer the right of immediate dismissal if the actor was deemed "unsatisfactory" for any reason.

By 1917, producers had agreed to a basic contract that limited the amount of unpaid rehearsal time for straight plays to four weeks and guaranteed actors at least two weeks' salary even if the show for which they rehearsed never opened. For actors in musicals, unpaid rehearsal time could run to six weeks.

In 1919, this contract was revised and renegotiated. Equity asked that the number of performances each week be limited to eight and demanded that actors who played extra performances be paid for them. From today's perspective, these demands are quite reasonable, but the producers refused to sign the new contract. On August 6, the actors went on strike, something the producers never believed they would do. The strike closed most theaters in New York and throughout the nation and also divided the theatrical community between those who believed in the actors' cause and those who did not. The majority, however, favored the actors.

When the strike was settled one month later, Actors' Equity had established itself as the bargaining agent for all actors. Of more long-term importance, the success of the strike paved the way for a dramatic change in the entire business of theater. Actors had rights and they had exercised them. The momentum engendered by the Actors' Equity strike led to the situation where today practically each person who works in the theater, is a member of a trade union or professional society.

These unions have a lot to say, for better or worse, about how the commercial theater operates. Practically every foreseeable situation is covered by a union rule or regulation. There are specific requirements for crews shooting film or video tape of theatrical productions to air over television. (Television critics normally include in their review a brief film clip of the show. A similar clip might be aired in conjunction with a star's guest appearance on an interview show.) There are rules that specify not only the length of time a crew can actually film in the theater but how many minutes can be aired, where in the theater the crews may film and the number of times a crew can film without the producer's paying special fees to stagehands and actors. The theatrical unions require twenty-four-hour written notification before a film crew is permitted into the theater. Special permission is required for a crew to use the theater's electricity and plug equipment into its outlets.

ATPAM (the Association of Theatrical Press Agents and Managers), to which press agents, company managers, and house managers belong, is a typical theater union. Affiliated with the American Federation of Labor, it has only about five hundred members. Potential members go through a lengthy and often arduous apprenticeship to get into ATPAM. The apprenticeship consists of working for a press agent or manager over three Broadway seasons and accumulating twenty weeks a year of apprenticeship credit. An apprentice can, if fortunate, obtain forty of these weeks in one season. But it is more usual for three seasons to be needed for a potential member to complete the apprenticeship. Although exceptions are sometimes made, an apprenticeship must be completed within five years. As most shows do not run for twenty weeks, it is often difficult to accumulate the weeks of employment credit necessary to complete the apprenticeship. One press agent tells this story:

"When I decided I wanted to be a theatrical press agent and get into ATPAM, I was lucky enough to get a job in an office which was handling a play where the senior press agent was willing to sponsor me as an apprentice.

"In September, which is when the union screens apprentice candidates, I went to the union and had an interview with the apprentice committee. Only five apprentices are accepted each year and I was lucky enough to be one of them. I signed an apprentice contract for the show I was working on. It turned out to be a hit and I was able to get two seasons of credit (40 weeks) that first year.

"However, the office I was with did not get any new plays to handle, which meant I had to get work with another press agent who had plays and was willing to put me on contract and didn't have another apprentice (a senior press agent is allowed to sponsor only one apprentice at a time). This is harder than it sounds. A lot of press agents won't hire apprentices. They don't have enough work themselves to be able to afford the union minimum apprentice salary and the thing about the theater is that it is always easy for you to get someone to come and work for hardly any money. People are dying to get into the theater and will do anything to get work in a theatrical office. It's a real hand-to-mouth existence. Most people think that this is true only for actors, but the fact is, it's that way for everyone. You never know if your play is going to run or not.

"It seemed that every time someone was willing to sign me on as an apprentice, the play would close. I had to get those last twenty weeks and it just didn't seem to be happening. I almost gave up. As a matter of fact, a lot of people do give up. They discover they can make a lot more money in other areas of publicity, have some stability in their lives and not work nearly as hard.

"However, I finally got into ATPAM. I think I worked on five different plays that season in three different offices just to complete those twenty weeks. It was really very hard. You really have to want it very much to put up with all that. I kept thinking that none of this has anything to do with whether I'm good or not. So much of it is luck. If the play ran, I got my credit. If it didn't, I was out."

Contracts

Contracts basically define payments and other legal obligations. In the theater, people receive payment in one of four ways: salary, fee, royalty (percentage), or a combination of royalty and fee. A salary is a weekly sum of money paid to an employee from which federal, state, and city taxes are deducted, along with Social Security and unemployment tax payments. A fee is a set sum of money received for specific services. The recipient is called an independent contractor. Taxes and other payments are not deducted but must be paid at tax time by the recipient. A royalty is a payment based upon a percentage of total receipts. In the theater, this usually means total weekly box office receipts.

Payments based upon percentages extend beyond income made by the Broadway or off-Broadway production. The life of most Broadway shows continues after Broadway. There can be a motion picture; a television special; a cast recording; a film cast recording; stock, dinner, and amateur theater productions; touring companies; and foreign productions. It is not unheard of for a play actually to lose money on Broadway and eventually make profits for everyone based on such subsidiary or secondary uses of the property.

Contract negotiation is a delicate business. Salary and fee payments serve to reduce the precious capital needed to maintain a production, especially just after opening when it is trying to build an audience. A fraction of a percentage point in a royalty payment can mean an enormous amount of money. As an example, the first contract signed is usually with the author or playwright. If the work is in the public domain—meaning that it is an old property and no person, estate, or organization legally holds the rights to it—anyone can produce without permission and no one receives any author's royalties. All of William Shakespeare's works are in the public domain. However, most of the time a contract must be signed between the author (or, where the author is dead, those handling the estate) and the producer. *Peter Pan*, one of the most frequently revived and best-loved plays, is based on a book by Sir James M. Barrie and was first produced in London in 1904. It was brought to Broadway a year later. The role of Peter Pan has been a favorite of many actresses, including Glynis Johns, Maggie Smith, Eva LeGallienne, Jean Arthur and, of course, Mary Martin, who with Cyril Ritchard starred in a 1954 full musical production. In 1979 it was again revived on Broadway, with Sandy Duncan in the starring role. All royalties earned by the author from the production go to the Hospital for Sick Children of London, as directed by Sir James Barrie in his will.

Most theater jobs are paid by weekly salaries, which are determined by negotiations between the League of New York Theatres and Producers and the various unions. The company manager, the press agent, most of the actors, and the personnel who work in the theater itself—ushers, ticket takers, treasurers, etc.—receive salaries and are not normally among those who actually share in profits or percentages of box office receipts or subsidiary rights. Usually, royalties are negotiated for those who have actually had a part in creating the show. The Dramatists Guild represents the playwright, or, in the case of a musical, the author of the "book"—the librettist—the composer, and the lyricist. Standard Guild terms provide a good example of how royalties and percentages work.

Like all unions and professional societies, the Guild was founded to correct certain unfair labor practices. In the early part of the century, when many more plays were produced each year and producers often had several productions going at once, they employed dramatists as "house writers." A writer was paid between $25 and $35 a week as long as the play ran. When it closed, the writer received nothing. If a movie sale was made or a foreign production was done, all profits went to the owner of the play—the producer. Stock production royalties and amateur rights were also held entirely by the producer. In addition, a playwright had no control over what he or she had written. The work could be completely rewritten, and the author had no say over the choice of director or actors.

In 1925, a group of thirty-two dramatists got together and agreed to withhold their plays from producers until a basic agreement was signed. Their proposed agreement guaranteed playwrights royalties and a participation in all subsidiary profits. It also stated that playwrights were to retain control over the ways in which their works were produced, giving them some say as to who could direct or act in their productions. Their aim was to get producers to recognize the rights of the playwrights and to sign the agreement. By 1927, over one hundred dramatists had pledged to withhold their scripts. A committee was formed to draw up the agreement. Among those on the committee was a young, relatively unknown playwright, Eugene O'Neill.

Today, the Dramatists Guild sets the minimum standards between producer and playwright for Broadway production. Even if a show outside of Guild jurisdiction is produced in New York (as in the case of a show being brought over from Great Britain), the terms would be relatively the same since most nations have the equivalent of a Dramatists Guild in order to protect their playwrights and authors. The contract determines minimum percentages and royalties an author must receive and states that the subsidiary rights basically belong to the author. However, once a play does open on Broadway and runs for a specified number of performances—twenty-one, to be exact—the producer and production company become vested with an interest in the rights, participating in any profits that might be made from sources other than the Broadway production.

Producers who option a property for Broadway receive the power to exercise first-class production rights. Beyond the Broadway production, these also include first-class touring companies, which play on the road throughout the country. Generally, first class means a company of Equity actors who play in first-class legitimate theaters (e.g., Boston's Colonial, Los Angeles' Shubert) in major cities of the United States, or bring the show to Great Britain within six months after the Broadway production has closed.

Usually writers of a straight play receive 5 percent of the first $5,000 in weekly box office receipts; 7 percent of the next $2,000; and 10 percent of everything over that. Writers for musical shows usually get 6 percent of the weekly box office receipts. For *Annie*, the agreement with Thomas Meehan, librettist; Charles Strouse, composer; and Martin Charnin, lyricist, called for the three to split 7.25 percent of the weekly gross receipts—as of the fall of 1979, about $42,000—of all United States companies.

Income from subsidiary rights involves even more money. By the fall of 1979, *Annie's* backers had received a 256.25 percent return on their original $800,000 investment, a total of $4,100,000. The *Annie* production company receives 40 percent of all *Annie* productions and merchandise. As of the fall of 1979, it had received $115,000 from a Christmas television special, $161,789 from the London production; and $117,434 from other foreign productions. The company will receive at least 83.5 million as its share of the $9.5 million sale of the film rights to Columbia Pictures.

However, these are figures for blockbuster successes. Royalty deals mean nothing most of the time as most Broadway shows do not make money. Even those that open and enjoy a decent run often don't bring in profit over a short term. When producers feel the show has a chance but needs time to build up an audience, they will ask playwrights, directors, and all others who are receiving box office percentages to suspend or take a cut in these

payments. And people usually do, knowing that any extra money is needed for additional advertising and promotion and even, at times, to pay the show's weekly operating costs.

Billing

Contracts do not mean just money. People want to be noticed and will sometimes give up money in exchange for billing. Billing is the prominence of one's name in all printed material about the show—the program, the front of the theater, advertisements, press releases, and posters. Contract negotiation includes how the name is to be used— whether it is above the title of the show; below the title with a box around it; in large type; in bold type; with a preface saying "and"; or below all the featured players on a special line which says "also starring."

The size of billing is specified as a percentage. The title of the production is 100 percent, and all names or titles on a billing page of the program or a billing box in front of the theater or in an advertisement are a percentage of the title. Besides the size of the billing, contracts also spell out when billing must be given. During the run of Edward Albee's

Reid Shelton, Andrea McArdle and Sandy starred in the original cast of *Annie*, the 1977 season's hit musical. This award-winning show has become one of the theater's most profitable productions, generating a best selling and award-winning cast album; four national companies; a London production; a record-breaking movie sale; a television special and many *Annie* products. These are subsidiary rights which involve all uses of a show beyond Broadway and can mean big money for investors and producers. *Photo by Martha Swope* last Broadway play, every time the name of the play was used, Albee's name had to be placed above the title and in the same size type (100 percent). Set and costume designers often have in their contracts a clause stating that every single time the director's name is used, their names must be included as well, in the same size type—usually 50 percent (one half the size of the title).

Billing is very important for all people in the theater. As a stage manager said: "Billing is the only way your name gets spread around. It's a way of being recognized and known. Once you're established and have a name, you want it out there." For an actor, billing determines dressing room location (those on stage level are most desirable) and often even the order of curtain calls. It is not uncommon at the end of the show for the star to appear alone at the last curtain call. Not always, but often, this is part of an actor's contract. Some actors' contracts contain approval of all photographs and publicity releases, dressers, and hairstylists and call for transportation to and from the theater.

Star billing—an actor's name above the title—means that the actor is just as important as the show. This usually means that the name itself will sell tickets. However, producers often give billing in lieu of money. Billing can get so complicated that a producer will often insist that the cast, or most members, accept a "favored nations" clause in their contracts. This clause stipulates that no one person receives more money or more visual prominence than another. The names of all performers are listed alphabetically.

There are numerous stories about billing. In 1937, *Red,*

A billing page from the *Annie* playbill. The size and boldness of type is determined by contract.

ALVIN THEATRE
UNDER THE DIRECTION OF THE MESSRS. NEDERLANDER
MILTON M. POLLACK, MANAGER

7 TONY AWARDS - INCLUDING BEST MUSICAL
N.Y. DRAMA CRITICS' CIRCLE AWARD - BEST MUSICAL
1978 GRAMMY AWARD

MIKE NICHOLS
Presents

A New Musical

Produced by
IRWIN MEYER   STEPHEN R. FRIEDMAN   LEWIS ALLEN

Book by   Music by   Lyrics by
THOMAS MEEHAN   CHARLES STROUSE   MARTIN CHARNIN
Starring
ALLISON   JOHN
SMITH   SCHUCK

KATHRYN   GARY
BOULÉ   And   BEACH

ALICE GHOSTLEY

With
RAYMOND THORNE   RITA RUDNER

JENNINE	TIFFANY	STACEY LYNN	MARTHA	CAROLINE	TARA
BABO	BLAKE	BRASS	BYRNE	DALY	KENNEDY

EDWIN BORDO   SHELLY BURCH   DICK ENSSLEN   TIMOTHY JECKO   R. MARTIN KLEIN
LARRY ROSS   MARIANNE SANAZARO   DONNA THOMASON   HENRIETTA VALOR   RICHARD WALKER

Settings by   Costumes by   Lighting by
DAVID MITCHELL   THEONI V. ALDREDGE   JUDY RASMUSON

Musical Direction   Dance Music   Orchestrations   Production
by   Arranged by   by   Stage Manager
ARNOLD GROSS   PETER HOWARD   PHILIP J. LANG   BROOKS FOUNTAIN

Musical Numbers Choreographed by
PETER GENNARO
Entire Production Directed by
MARTIN CHARNIN

Based on LITTLE ORPHAN ANNIE. *
By Permission of Chicago Tribune — New York News Syndicate, Inc.

Produced by
ALVIN NEDERLANDER   THE JOHN F. KENNEDY CENTER   ICARUS
ASSOCIATES, INC.   FOR THE PERFORMING ARTS   PRODUCTIONS

Produced in Association with PETER CRANE
Original Cast Recording Available On Columbia Records & Tapes

Originally Produced by THE GOODSPEED OPERA HOUSE
MICHAEL P. PRICE, Executive Producer

Hot and Blue, a musical by Cole Porter, Howard Lindsay, and Russel Crouse opened. It starred Ethel Merman and Jimmy Durante and featured a young, not yet very well-known actor, Bob Hope. Both Merman and Durante had been promised star billing and neither was willing to relinquish first position. The compromise became one of the theater's most memorable billing arrangements.

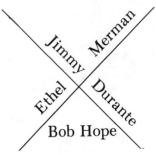

In 1958, two stars, Charles Boyer and Claudette Colbert, appeared in a show, *Marriage-Go-Round*. Both stars insisted upon top billing in the playbill. The cover consisted of a photograph of each. The left-hand position is top billing. As both stars couldn't occupy the same space at once, two separate playbills were printed with Boyer occupying the left position in one and Colbert in the other. Each week, a different playbill was distributed so each star could receive top billing every other week. On opening night, the two sets of playbills were given to the audience.

More recently, a billing dispute occurred around *Sweeney Todd: The Demon Barber Of Fleet Street*, winner of the 1978 Tony Award for Best Musical. *Sweeney Todd* first appeared in London as a straight play in 1972. It had

The houseboard for *The Elephant Man* is mounted in front of the Booth Theater. Theatrical unions require a houseboard to be placed outside each theater, listing those who contractually receive billing in a specific size and typeface.   *Photo by Roger Greenawalt*

been adapted by Christopher Bond from a nineteenth-century melodrama. American producers optioned Bond's play for Broadway development and brought in Hugh Wheeler to adapt the script for the musical stage.

Part of Bond's contract stipulated that he was to receive billing 50 percent the size and prominence of Stephen Sondheim's, *Sweeney Todd's* composer and lyricist. After the Broadway opening and success of the production, Bond's agent protested that not only was his name on the playbill and outside the theater less than half the size of Sondheim's but in such light type as to be barely noticeable. The situation was corrected. Such is the stuff that theatrical law suits are made of. Billing is therefore monitored as carefully as money.

Acting in the Theater: Rewards and Riches

Casting

To fill the available roles in a theatrical production, most Broadway producers use casting directors. Their job is to find actors and actresses who might be right for roles in the show and present them to those who actually do the hiring: director, producer and playwright. For the actor, an interview with a casting director is often the first step toward a part. There will be more interviews, auditions, callbacks, and ultimately either a part or, more frequently, a thank you and rejection.

Since most casting directors not only cast for theatrical productions but for movies and television as well, they see literally hundreds of actors each year. They are in a position to know not only the quality of an actor's work, but also an actor's development over a period of time.

The process of casting begins as soon as the producer begins work on a show. The producer, director, and playwright meet with the casting director to discuss and analyze the qualities required for the various roles. The casting director prepares composites that are minidescriptions of each featured role, detailing physical type, personality characteristics, and special quirks. The casting director also studies the interrelationships of the roles. Just as certain aspects of the show begin to come to life when the general manager starts to work on the production's budget, a similar thing happens as casting is discussed. The characters in the play emerge as individual personalities who must relate to one another.

Casting directors for theatrical productions rarely do the actual hiring (those who work for the television stations and advertising agencies that produce soap operas and commercials often do). Unlike agents, who represent actors and actresses directly, casting directors do not receive commissions or a percentage of the salaries from those for whom they obtain work. Casting directors are paid a fee or royalty by the production company.

Thousands of actors are always looking for work. One of the ways in which they do so is by trying to get casting directors to see them. So, in addition to the actual work of casting for specific projects, a casting director is inundated by actors calling for interviews, dropping off pictures and resumes, and requesting attendance at dramatic workshops and productions. One New York casting director who is particularly sensitive to the needs and feelings of actors says: "Sometimes I hear myself and I can't believe it! No matter how much you care, it's impossible to treat actors individually. Sometimes I am so quick and abrupt that I cannot believe that it's me talking."

Even a production that seems simple to cast requires intuition and skill in finding the right combination of actors. For instance, Neil Simon's musical *They're Playing Our Song* starred Lucie Arnaz and Robert Klein. The casting director was asked to find two actors with recognizable names but not superstar status (the producers wanted actors who would remain with the show for a reasonable length of time). Over a thousand were screened for the two available parts. For the original production of *My Fair Lady*, more than five thousand singers auditioned for the chorus before the final fifteen were selected. When off-Broadway's longest-running show, *Vanities*, decided to screen possible replacements for its three actresses, more than eighteen hundred photos and résumés were received within the first week following the announcement.

Not all roles are filled with the help of a casting director. A big star does not go to auditions. The star's agent or lawyer is usually contacted by the producer. However, most of the time—and this is true even for those who play featured (speaking) roles and are fairly well known—it is the actor who must impress the playwright, the director, and the producer.

Working in the Theater

Actors' Equity, the union for all performers in the legitimate theater, has about 28,000 members. An actor must be a member of Equity to perform in the legitimate theater. It is estimated that less than a third of the members of Equity work regularly, and that their median income is about $8,000 a year. Equity reports an 80% unemployment rate at any given time.

So fierce is the competition for jobs in the theater that it is very difficult for foreign actors to work in the United States. Alan Ayckbourn's London hit comedy *Bedroom Farce* opened on Broadway in 1979. It was written by England's leading comedy writer, who has often been referred to as the English Neil Simon. Alan Ayckbourn has had other shows on Broadway, including *Absurd Person Singular* and *The Norman Conquests*, which was later filmed and produced for the Public Broadcasting Service and seen over nationwide television. All of the plays had American actors.

However, for *Bedroom Farce*, a special arrangement was made with Actors' Equity to allow the British company to open the production on Broadway. The actors were permitted to perform for a limited amount of time after which they were replaced by American actors. Of course, British Equity, Great Britain's theatrical union, is as protective of British actors as Actors' Equity is of American actors. When *A Chorus Line* was produced in London, its producers wanted Donna McKechnie, the American star of the show, to repeat her role in Great Britain. After much negotiation back and forth, British Equity would not allow her to perform the role, stating that it would take work away from an equally talented and qualified British actress.

So, from the beginning, an actor in the theater must realize what the odds are. Many start careers as actors and eventually abandon them. Even for those with talent, success depends upon an inordinate amount of luck and an aggressive temperament to spend the amount of time and energy necessary simply to get into the position where there might be work.

The type of aggressiveness necessary to succeed is, in many ways, incompatible with the actor personality. The now classic film *All About Eve*, starring Bette Davis, was later produced as a Broadway musical, *Applause*, starring Lauren Bacall, who won a Tony Award for her performance. *All About Eve* portrays a young ingenue who methodically and maliciously plays on an aging film star to catapult herself to success. There are, of course, stars who have always been unwavering in their pursuit of fame and stardom, driven more by the desire for success than love of acting. However, while any honest actor will admit to wanting stardom and celebrity, most enter the theater because they derive genuine satisfaction from the very process of acting. As one actor says: "Where else can you get paid to pretend you are someone other than yourself? I constantly learn who I am by portraying other people's fantasies."

The business of theater—auditions, hustling, trying to impress, constant attempts to be seen, and almost continual rejection—are often excruciatingly difficult for the very type of person who decides to act on the stage. However, many actors manage to stay with it. Most actors are careerists—not stars. As one actor said: "People don't realize that you can work as an actor and not be a star. If you say you're an actor to most people and they don't know your name or your face, you're not an actor to them. But you can make money and you can work. You always try to get jobs that involve real acting. If you are willing to compromise and are able to hustle and always know what is around, you can make it as a professional and still act."

Being Seen

For a beginning actor, the most important goal is to be seen by the right people. The right people are those who hire. Basically, this means that the actor must be asked to audition. This doesn't sound so difficult but, in reality, it is one of the hardest steps in an actor's career.

How does an actor get to be seen? Everyone has a different story. One actor, who now lives and works in New York, started off in Chicago after coming there from his home town of Peoria, Illinois: "I went to high school in Peoria and knew that I wanted to act. I went to Northwestern in Evanston and studied drama. After graduation,

I auditioned for the American Troupe of College Players, where I spent the summer in Denver acting. I loved it and decided I wanted to be a professional and really thought about how I was going to do it.

"I knew I wanted to come to New York—that's where the action is—but I decided I'd better be a professional first and that meant getting my union card. You just don't walk into New York and get on the Broadway stage unless you're Lawrence Olivier.

"I went back to Chicago. The competition is not as fierce there. If you're any good, you're going to work in Chicago. A friend of mine from Peoria got me into an audition for a dinner theater in Omaha. The people who ran it were in Chicago to audition actors. They loved me but didn't hire me. That's one thing you have to get used to in this business. Sometimes, you know you're good and they think so, too, but they just can't use you then. But, two months later, they called.

"I got my Equity card and for seven months had a wonderful time playing roles in A Funny Thing Happened on the Way to the Forum, South Pacific and Hair. I wanted that card because I knew it would help me get an agent.

"After seven months, I went back to Chicago. I had no work. That's another thing you have to get used to if you're an actor . . . not working. You really have to learn to handle it. I decided I'd better get an agent and I did, literally by walking around banging on doors. That's something you can still do in Chicago. He got me a job in an industrial show, where I met a lot of New York actors. They were all represented by one agent. One day that agent flew out to Chicago to see them all. I went up to him and introduced myself and told him that I was definitely coming to New

York and asked if he would represent me when I did. He said that he would.

"I worked around Chicago for a while and then went to New York to audition for some soaps and the revival of *My Fair Lady*. My Chicago agent had set them up. I called one of my New York friends whom I had met at the industrial and she called up the agent to remind him about me and I signed on with him. I then decided to stay in New York."

This actor went on to play one of the leads in the 1976 revival of *Hair* and is now in a position where he is regularly called for auditions.

Without doubt, the most important task for any actor (with the exception of the fortunate few who, as mentioned, are in that rare position where they are sought after), is to know what is going on in the business. Actors must always know what shows are auditioning; what productions are in the planning process; what shows are seeking replacements; which out-of-town regional companies are casting; what stock, road, or bus and truck productions are in formation. In short, they must know where the work is or will be.

There are several ways of keeping themselves informed. The three theatrical trade publications, *Show Business*, *Backstage*, and *Variety*, list all auditions and productions that are casting. These weekly publications, particularly *Backstage*, are sources of possible employment. They are regular reading for actors. In addition, actors exchange information. In the theatrical community, everyone talks. An actor seeking work will start building a communications network comprised of others who are also trying to get their foot in the door. Although it is likely that information is sometimes purposely withheld (particularly by an actor

CASTING NEWS

BROADWAY

"A Life" (P.). Available parts: male, understudy, early 60s, retirement age, intellectual, snobbish, aloof, cruel, sarcastic, scholarly; femme, 60, understudy, limps slightly from accident, spunky, great individuality, very outspoken, not intelligent but not stupid, more physical than intellectual, good sense of humor; male, understudy, early 60s, feckless, goodhumored, physically gone to seed, big man, enjoys pleasures of life, grey or white hair, not intelligent, tender-hearted, messes everything up; femme, 60, understudy, natural gaiety, under which is a terror of her husband's displeasure, intelligent, book-oriented, shy, soft spoken, tender, forgiving timid, foolish, devoted; young men, 17-20; and young femmes, 17-20. Equity principal interviews being held next Monday (21), Tuesday (22) and July 24 from 10:20 a.m. to 5:30 p.m., each day, at the Equity Audition Center (165 West 46th St., N.Y.).

"Annie" (M). For possible future replacements in all companies. Available parts: Daddy Warbucks understudy, 45-50, business tycoon, elegant, masculine, should be a big, well-built man, must sing exceptionally well, high-baritone or tenor, to an F; Franklin Delano Roosevelt, 40-50, must be a very good actor, should be able to believably impersonate Roosevelt during the Depression era, baritone, must be able to sing a patter

next Tuesday (22), Wednesday (23) and July 24 from 10 a.m. to 1 p.m. and 2-6 p.m. each day at Actors' Equity Interview and Audition Center (165 West 46th St., N.Y.).

"Passione" (P). Available parts: male, understudy, mid-50s, reasonably tall, heavy-set and bald, lively manner and charming, has retained a certain Italianate handsomeness and robustness; male, an old man of 80, very thin, almost skeletal, not quite lucid, but very lively and sprightly, speaks mostly Italian and some very broken English; femme, understudy, late 40s-early 50s, striking and handsome who has aged considerably better than her former husband, reserved manner and shy, overt warmth, genuine sensitivity; femme, understudy, late 40s-early 50s, a muscular, rather leathery woman, abrasive manner, straight-forward and frank; male, understudy, early 50s, slick, a good talker, very charming and a professional hustler, bookie, fence and slightly shady mover, snazzy dresser, handsome and sexy; male, understudy, 30; femme, understudy, 29, she is very beautiful. Equity principal interviews being held next Wednesday (23), July 25 and 28 from 10 a.m. to 1 p.m. and from 2-6 p.m., at Equity Audition Center (165 West 46th St., N.Y.).

"Piaf" (M). Show is performed by cast of 14 actors and two musicians playing some 31 characters, representing the various personal who views another actor as a possible competitor), word of mouth is rampant. News of new productions, names of possible contacts, out-of-town casting calls, all travel very quickly along the theater circuit.

By Equity rule, all Broadway and off-Broadway productions have what are called Equity Principal Interviews (E.P.I.s) which are just what the term implies: brief, three-minute interviews at which the actor has the opportunity to be seen by the show's director or casting director and to hand over his picture or résumé. An E.P.I. is not an audition but is the first step in a process whereby an actor may actually be called back for a formal audition. Opinions vary as to whether anyone really gets a role by attending such an interview. Technically, an E.P.I. is for Equity members exclusively. However, non-Equity members will often be seen at the end of the E.P.I. after the actual members have been seen. And, as happens often in the theater, there are cases of an unknown getting a part through an E.P.I. So, most beginning actors—Equity or non-Equity—do go to E.P.I.s, at least when they are starting out.

As one actress, speaking of her first off-Broadway role, said: "Someone suggested I go in and wait until everyone had been seen. Sometimes the stage manager says you can be seen and sometimes not. I waited all day and was the last person seen. The next day, they called me and asked me to sing and I got the job. That's how I got my Equity card."

One of the reasons off-off-Broadway flourishes in New

Casting calls in *Variety*, the weekly show business trade publication. These are notices of all Broadway, off-Broadway, showcase and out-of-town productions that are auditioning and casting actors for roles.

York is because many of these productions are "showcases" in which actors will work for no pay. There is a special performance code that showcase productions must adhere to under an agreement with Actors' Equity. From an actor's point of view, these showcases provide a place to invite agents and casting directors—another opportunity to be seen.

The best place to be seen, of course, is in a Broadway or off-Broadway play. One actress, who appeared in a Broadway musical that opened and closed on the same night, said, "There were two weeks of previews. The producer— I'll always love him for this—gave us permission to invite anyone we wanted for those two weeks. I invited everyone. People will come to see you on Broadway although they might not come to a showcase. What it meant was that no important casting person can tell me that they don't know my work. It was so frustrating not being able to get into those auditions. No matter what my agent said (and he did get me that part) . . . 'she's so great' . . . 'she's just perfect' . . . the casting directors would usually say that they didn't want to see me. They didn't know me and they've got a list of people. The one that cast that show—now I'm on her list. I'm not a nobody."

This actress probably benefited more from her one-night stand than she would have if the show had run. She used those two weeks of previews to be seen and she got some good reviews on opening night. When the show closed, she followed up every opportunity and pursued every new contact she made. She was "hot" and "new" following that show and, as she says: "The star was coming back to Broadway after having had some bad luck professionally. She really needed a hit. I didn't. I really needed to be seen."

And, of course, one must always remember that there are virtually no overnight successes. This actress got her Broadway part after almost six years of working out of town in dinner theaters, small regional companies, and summer stock. The actor from Peoria got his chance after working for three years in various jobs in Chicago and also around the country. There does seem to be an unofficial apprenticeship that most actors must serve. Actors themselves refer to "paying your dues." Even if they are based in New York, they must work out of town. They must build on those contacts and experiences to get their Equity card and the right kind of agent, who can provide entry to the right casting directors and the right auditions.

Agents

Most actors believe that it is important, at least in the beginning, to have an agent. An agent is franchised by one of the dramatic unions and functions as an employment agency for actors. The agent must also have a license from the state labor commission to practice. Actors signing with an agent agree to allow the agent to be their exclusive representative in a specific area of the business and to pay a commission to the agent on any money received through the agent's efforts. This commission usually amounts to 10 percent, although it can vary. If an actor is in an off-Broadway play and is receiving an off-Broadway minimum salary, Equity requires that the agent receive only 5 percent.

There is no hard and fast rule for getting an agent. Actors used to get agents by what was called making the rounds. Actors would literally go from door to door, carrying 8" × 10" glossy photographs of themselves with a résumé stapled to the back. They would return at a later time or call for an appointment. Usually, this entailed many visits and many calls before an appointment was arranged but, eventually, an agent would agree to see them.

Years ago, when most active producers maintained their own casting offices, young actors and actresses would visit a producer's office, hoping that there might be a small part in a road company or perhaps even a Broadway show. Even if there was no acting work, there was sometimes a messenger or office job available. Actors would do anything to be in the position to hear about and have access to work. Lauren Bacall started off working in the office of a producer. Wanting desperately to be in the theater, she went to the offices of the Shubert brothers hoping to get a job as an usher. In those days, ushers were not unionized and she got a job at the Morosco Theatre for $8 a week. It was the job she wanted, precisely because it would put her in a place where she would not only hear about available work but possibly meet those who could actually give her work.

Now, however, most agents keep their doors locked, as much a result of deteriorating safety and increased crime as anything else. A few have signs on their doors indicating the hours when aspiring actors can drop off photos and résumés. In addition, as agencies consolidate, creating large entertainment complexes, there are fewer individual agents. The two largest, William Morris and International Creative Management (ICM), have comparatively tiny theater departments, reflecting the proportion of money involved in theater as opposed to film and television.

As in earlier times, an actor must persevere in trying to get an agent—calling to ask for an appointment, sending video-cassettes of any film or television work, inviting potential agents to see live appearances. Personal contacts are important and it really helps to be recommended by someone. Using a name familiar to an agent makes a big difference in having your call returned. "I would say," says one actress, "that if the percentages were known, probably the most important way is through friends."

An agent can be very helpful in arranging for young actors to get into auditions. Casting directors frequently ask agents to refer people who might be right for a particular role. Agents do not work only for theater. They are able to get jobs for industrial shows, soap operas, and commercials. An agent can open doors that are closed to an individual acting on his or her own.

However, once actors are in a position to pick and choose, they will frequently terminate the association with the agent or seek representation from a number of agents. One actress says: "I have several agents. I have one who represents me for theater; another for television; and another who sends me up for industrials and commercials." Another actor says: "I've finally reached the point where I can make money for an agent. I can work, not necessarily on the stage which is what I really want, but there is work for me in commercials, industrials, and even on the soaps if I want it. Agents call me and ask to send me to an audition because they know that the casting directors know me and there is a good chance I will get the part."

But this works only for a while. As soon as actors start working with regularity and no longer necessarily for minimum salaries, a relationship with one agent is resumed. The agent not only will be called about work for the client but will become a negotiator, handling salary, fee, and other contractual details. At a certain point, an agent becomes necessary, not only to obtain work but to act as middleman between actor and producer, be it for television, film, or theater.

Making a Living

Once actors have access to work, they can pursue an acting career. That means they don't have to give up. At this point, actors are faced with different and possibly even worse frustrations. They have made real sacrifices, both personal and financial, up to now.

By this time, they may have or may be thinking about starting a family. Or they may be fed up with sharing an apartment, living in a dark, small, inadequate space, and possibly spending most of their working time on the road. The almost constant rejection at auditions—"we love you but you're not right"; "there might be something in a few months"—and the constant hustling for work can become truly demoralizing.

For many, work in the theater becomes the gravy, the icing on the cake. After the euphoria of realizing that they are at least getting into the auditions and getting roles some of the time, comes a kind of crisis. Some, at this point, leave. Occasionally, they have the opportunity to return.

Gerald Hiken came to New York from his hometown of Milwaukee over thirty years ago. He studied at the Actors Studio and gained a reputation in theatrical circles as an actor of tremendous range and skill. He appeared in productions that are still talked about today. An "actor's actor"—a term meaning, in truth, that he was an artistic success but not a financial success—Hiken found that in order to make money, he was always forced to accept roles that called for someone "genial, plump, and balding."

After spending over ten years on the New York stage, he married and started a family and decided that the business of making a living in New York was simply too frustrating. The roles that gave him money, he didn't like. Those roles he liked were not in productions that paid. He moved to northern California, where he founded a repertory theater. Then he teamed up with another actor and traveled throughout the country doing a two-man show, mostly of original material. To support his growing family, Hiken accepted television work (available in California and not in New York) and acted when he could in the kinds of productions he found satisfying. There was never much money, but Palo Alto is not New York and living is both less expensive and less difficult. A few seasons ago he returned briefly to New York, as Anne Bancroft's husband in *Golda*, not the type of role he was particularly comfortable in.

In the spring of 1979, Hiken received a call from the Chelsea Theater Center. They offered him the lead role in a new play called *Strider*. It was to be a limited three-week engagement and the salary $200 a week. Hiken left his family in California and came to New York. However, when *Strider* opened, it received wonderful reviews and Hiken himself got notices like "A special bravo—no, a fusillade of bravos—is due to Gerald Hiken as Strider. Hiken is giving one of the most remarkable performances I have ever had the fortune to see" (Clive Barnes, *New York Post*) . . . "Not since Zero Mostel's *Rhinoceros* has an actor been so magnificently transmogrified. . . . Gerald Hiken is gloriously triumphant" (Mel Gussow, *The New York Times*). When *Strider* moved to Broadway, Hiken received star billing above the title and was nominated for a Tony Award.

This opportunity for commercial *and* artistic success took over thirty years to achieve and, as Hiken says: "I'm not going in this all twirly-eyed. I know that when this is over, I probably won't work again for a long time. I know how hard it is."

For the actor who does want to continue in the theater,

however, New York remains the place to be. Even auditions for out-of-town work are held in New York. You don't travel to Cincinnati's Playhouse in the Park or Houston's Alley Theatre to audition. Usually, out-of-town productions send representatives to New York and hold auditions in the city. The bus and truck companies and national touring companies of Broadway shows are all organized in New York.

In New York, aside from the numerous restaurants that are staffed by out-of-work actors (that group still in the first stage of their career and still trying to be seen), there are really two ways for actors to support themselves: commercials and daytime television, or soaps. Most film and television work originates and is produced on the West Coast, although recently an increasing number of feature films are being shot in New York City. Few actors, though, are successful enough to move back and forth between jobs on both coasts. Just as to work in the theater means to live in New York, working in film and television means living in California. Most must live where the work is.

In 1980, only two soap operas—"Days of Our Lives" and "General Hospital"—were not filmed in New York. The producers of soap operas are aware that many of their actors are primarily interested in theater. They are accommodating about taping and rehearsals, and acting classes. While some actors feel that daytime television is so without any redeeming qualities that they would rather starve than appear on the soaps, for many daytime television provides a fairly steady source of income and the opportunity not only to act, but to gain experience as well. For a beginning actor, the soaps provide another opportunity to be seen. Always on the lookout for new faces, casting directors and agents do watch television.

Commercials also provide income and visibility. Cast by casting directors who work for the advertising agencies that produce them, commercials can provide a lucrative source of income. Actors receive not only a per diem or daily "session fee," but residuals. These are payments made each time the commercial is aired during the typical thirteen-week cycle that most commercials run. Actors can make a substantial income on a commercial that is televised nationally for several months.

Most successful stage actors who must support themselves and their families end up taking a variety of nontheatrical acting jobs. Frances Sternhagen, one of the most respected actresses on the stage today, has done it all. Married to an actor and the mother of six children, Ms. Sternhagen played a lead in *Equus* and in 1980 starred in *On Golden Pond*. A Tony Award winner for her role in Neil Simon's *The Good Doctor*, she has been nominated for a Tony four other times. In addition to her work on the stage, Ms. Sternhagen has appeared in films, including *Starting Over* with Burt Reynolds; on several daytime television series, including "Search for Tomorrow," "Love of Life," and "The Doctors"; and was seen nationally in a Colgate commercial in which she portrayed Mrs. Marsh, the Colgate lady.

One of the most successful working actresses in the business, Ms. Sternhagen has reached that enviable position where work comes to her. She is able to maintain her home in a New York suburb, commuting to the theater or even back and forth to California when she is appearing in a film or television special. She regrets the current split between the theater and film and television. "When television was presented live from New York in the 1950s," she says, "we all worked on the shows and networks. It was TV at its best."

About doing commercials, Ms. Sternhagen says: "I don't know if any actor who really loves doing theater could say he loves doing commercials. But you have to think of it as money and an awful lot of actors do need money. What I have told young actors about doing commercials is, think of it as children's theater. If you're going to do *Peter Rabbit*, how are you going to do it as a grownup without feeling like an idiot? You have to say, 'I'm going to pretend that I love this product'—what's acting anyway? You have to act as if you're enjoying it. You do what you have to do."

The point is that with talent, perseverance, and a willingness to do what you have to do—and a certain amount of luck—a person can work successfully as an actor and derive great satisfaction from it.

Broadway Theaters:
The Right and Wrong Side
of the Street

There are forty-two legitimate Broadway theaters—or houses, as they are called in the business. The actual Broadway theater district extends from 41st Street, the site of the recently renovated Nederlander, to 53d Street, where the large 1,788-seat Broadway Theatre stands. The Vivian Beaumont, which is part of the Lincoln Center complex, uptown at 65th Street and Broadway, is included.

The three categories of theater that exist have been defined by Actors' Equity and the other theatrical unions for purposes of establishing minimum salaries, minimum number of employees per house, and other requirements for the productions that play in them. While most off-off-Broadway houses are not subject to union rules, it is likely that they will soon come under union jurisdiction since more and more members of Equity and other unions are working in them.

A house that seats up to 499 people is considered an off-Broadway theater except if it is located between 5th and 9th Avenues from 34th to 56th Street or from 56th to 72d Street between 5th Avenue and the Hudson River. An off-Broadway house has traditionally been rented on what is called a four-wall basis. This means that the producer simply leases the space and pays a weekly rent. The producer hires personnel to maintain the theater and man the box office. However, as off-Broadway theaters become more establishment and similar to the commercial Broadway theater, many of them now have regularly employed house managers and box office and maintenance staffs. Increasingly, it is only off-off-Broadway theaters that are rented on a four-wall basis.

A house with a capacity of more than 499 is classified as a Broadway house. A Broadway house is almost never rented on a four-wall basis. For each Broadway theater, a certain minimum number of personnel must be employed. The actual figure is negotiated and agreed upon by the various theatrical unions and the bargaining agent for producers and theater owners, the League of New York Theatres and Producers. Each house requires a certain number of stagehands and box office attendants. Theaters are also classified as musical or straight houses, although some are known as "swing houses" or "contract houses," and accommodate either type of production. The union specifies the number of musicians who must be hired for each musical house. In addition, some of the theaters classified as swing houses are required to pay a minimum number of musicians regardless of whether the theater houses a straight play or musical.

The third category of theater is the middle house, with a maximum of 499 seats but located in the Broadway area. Middle houses are considered by most standards to be Broadway houses. They charge considerably higher ticket prices than the few comparably sized off-Broadway houses, but lower prices than Broadway theaters. The unions specify contracts for cast and personnel which call for higher pay than off-Broadway and lower than Broadway . . . somewhere in the middle, hence the term "middle house."

Seventeen of Broadway's legitimate houses are owned or operated by the Shubert Organization. Named for the three Shubert brothers—Lee, Sam, and Jacob—the Shubert Organization is the single most powerful body in the commercial theater today, a distinction it has held almost since the turn of the century.

Raised in Syracuse, New York, the three brothers were the sons of a Russian immigrant who arrived in Syracuse in 1882. The father, an alcoholic, could not hold a job and the eldest son, Levi (whose name was later "Americanized" to Lee), started working at the age of ten, shining shoes and selling newspapers. The location that ten-year-old Lee picked was in front of the Wieting Theater, a decision that eventually molded the course of the American theater.

This was the period when the New York theater was beginning to have national impact. The actor/director/playwright-manager was gradually being replaced by manager/producers who mounted plays in New York City. If the plays were successful, the producers organized road companies and brought live theater to audiences throughout the nation. It was in this era that the power of the producer and theater owner emerged, a power they retain today.

The Shubert brothers were very ambitious and, having started with the Wieting, within a few years all three were working in enterprises that gradually spread into Syracuse's other theaters. By the end of the nineteenth century, the Shubert brothers were managing and booking attractions into theaters throughout upper New York State and New England. They had begun their ascendance as powers in the theater.

Maytime   Jan 14-1918

Sam S. Shubert Theatre

Forty Fourth
Street

West of
Broadway

SHUBERT THEATRICAL CO., Lessees

Under the direction of the MESSRS. SHUBERT

"Direct from New York" was the most important phrase a theater owner could use to attract audiences. Hundreds of theater owners vied for the most elaborate productions with the biggest "names" to play their theaters. Owners and managers often booked productions to play their theaters months in advance. To ensure that there would be a production, they often booked two shows for the same date, knowing that it was likely that one of the productions contracted would have closed on the road or be unable to arrive on time to fulfill the booking.

A troupe of actors often arrived in a small town on the afternoon of the evening performance. They would go to bed following the performance and wake up at 4:00 A.M. to catch a train to the next town. Often the company would arrive at the theater and discover, because of the common practice of double booking, another troupe setting up to present its show. These and other abuses which ultimately led to the stringent unionization of the theaters of today also paved the way for the stunning success of the Shuberts.

In 1895, a group of six businessmen joined together to create an organization that would coordinate theater bookings in New York and throughout the country. Called the Syndicate, it was managed by Abe Erlanger, one of the six founders. The Syndicate was established to plan and organize road tours. It was to book attractions, using a logical sequence of cities, and would guarantee individual theater owners that the production booked would arrive on the proper date. The formation of the Syndicate was hailed

The Sam Shubert Theater, constructed as a memorial to Sam Shubert by his brothers Lee and J. J., stands on the 44th Street end of Shubert Alley. Opened in 1913, the theater still houses the offices of the Shubert Organization on its upper floors. *Photo courtesy of Culver Pictures* by the press and theatrical community as a means toward ending the disorganization and unpredictability of the road and as protection for the numerous actors and other theater people traveling throughout the country in these small companies.

However, it soon became evident that, in a different way, the situation was even worse than it had been before the Syndicate was established. Theater owners paid a fee to the Syndicate when the show was booked into their theater. When the production actually played, the Syndicate received a percentage of the total box office receipts. This, in itself, was not unreasonable and is a practice still followed today. But the Syndicate insisted that theater owners sign exclusive contracts prohibiting any attractions not sponsored by the Syndicate from playing their theaters. Soon, the Syndicate had amassed such power that it was virtually impossible for stars or producers who refused to work with the Syndicate to play a Broadway theater or even to tour outside New York. The Syndicate thus had almost total power over all commercial theater.

It was rumored, as well, that certain drama writers and reviewers on newspapers throughout the country, were on the Syndicate's payroll. Although probably few actual bribes were paid, critics were sometimes called in as "play consultants," creating a glaring conflict of interest. When it came time for these same critics to review the plays on which they had acted as "consultants," invariably the plays received favorable reviews.

In 1900, the Shuberts made their first foray into New York, determined to set up a rival booking agency to compete with the Syndicate. By this time, the Syndicate was hated and feared by most people in the theater, although few had the courage to speak out publicly against the organization. Their livelihood would be threatened if they did. The young Shubert brothers had many allies, but even they could not brook the power of the Erlanger empire.

In 1903, however, an event took place that began the Syndicate's downfall. There was a fire in Chicago's Iroquois Theatre, a Syndicate-owned house. It occurred during a holiday matinee performance of a popular play, *Mr. Bluebeard*, on December 30. The production was attended primarily by women and children. More than 600 people died.

Immediately, theaters throughout the nation were closed and new fire codes were written and established by law. Theaters that were too old to be renovated, many of which were owned or leased by the Syndicate, remained permanently closed, weakening the Syndicate's empire. In addition, newspapers and magazines, reflecting the popular outrage and shock at the tragedy, suddenly started to report on the Syndicate's enormous power and its abusive use of that power.

In a mood of accommodation, Sam Shubert met with Abe Erlanger a few days after the fire, offering him the use of the Shubert Theatre in Chicago until the Iroquois could be rebuilt. The Shuberts were hoping for an alliance. However, two weeks later, Erlanger decided that he neither wanted nor needed the Shubert. This so angered Sam that the Shuberts increased their activity, taking over theaters at an even greater pace. They were, of course, aided by the new problems confronting the Syndicate.

The rivalry continued for the next two years. The Shuberts became increasingly successful, although they still represented little real threat to Erlanger. But on May 11, 1905, a railroad car in which Sam Shubert was riding sideswiped another car carrying a large amount of dynamite.

A view of Broadway at 46th Street looking north in 1915.

Photo courtesy of Culver Pictures

Sam Shubert was mortally wounded in the terrible explosion. He died the next day.

Lee immediately took over the Shubert enterprise. He was so depressed by his brother's death that he decided to approach Erlanger again, to explore the possibility of the Syndicate's buying the Shubert business. Lee asked only that the Syndicate honor certain commitments made by Sam before his death. It is said that Erlanger's response was "I don't honor contracts with dead men." Lee, enraged, vowed to destroy Erlanger and the Syndicate.

Within a year, motivated as much by rage as ambition, the Shuberts owned—either totally or in part—more than 120 theaters throughout the United States. In their revenge, the two remaining Shuberts were aided by an extraordinary building boom around Times Square. Office buildings and theaters were under construction throughout the area, many built and owned by the Shuberts, others on long-term leases to them. The New York City subway system was under construction, its main terminus the 42d Street/ Times Square station. Eventually most of the individual subway lines serving the city converged there, making the area easily accessible to vast numbers of people. The New York City subway system did not then suffer the reputation it does today—it was safe, clean, and efficient. Grand Central Station and Pennsylvania Station, the railroad points of departure for all out-of-town tours, were located nearby. By the mid-1920s, more than seventy theaters in the Times Square/Broadway area offered live entertainment that ranged from quality legitimate plays to vaudeville and burlesque. Until 1950, the Shuberts owned or controlled a large proportion of all the theaters in the nation. Then the United States government brought an antitrust suit that forced the Shubert Organization to sell many theaters, including four in New York City.

Today, most of their New York theaters are in Broadway's prime theater location. The Shubert Theatre, which opened in 1913 in memory of Sam Shubert, houses *A Chorus Line*, which has played to full houses since its opening in 1975. The Shubert Organization maintains its offices above the theater, which is located on Shubert Alley, a pedestrian walk between 44th and 45th Streets. The business today is run by two former Shubert protégés, attorneys

A view of Broadway at 51st Street in 1933.

Photo courtesy of Culver Pictures

Gerald Schoenfeld and Bernard Jacobs. Under Schoenfeld and Jacobs, the Shubert Organization is still the most powerful organization in the commercial theater today.

Booking a Theater

Booking a theater is one of a producer's most delicate and important decisions. A production virtually never goes into rehearsal until the producer has a theater in which to open his production. Sometimes, if the production company has raised all of its money, the money will remain unused in a bank account until the producer has some firm assurance that a theater—and an acceptable one—is available. Occasionally, this even means postponing a show from one season to the next, and risking the loss of a star or key cast member.

Each Broadway house has its own personality, a special feel, to which producers respond. They try to match the intangible personality of the theater to the production. If a producer has had a failure in one house, even if it is perfect in both size and location, he may not want to use that theater again. Conversely, when a producer has had a hit at a certain house, he may have a special fondness for the theater and try to use it again.

Theater owners are also selective about what plays they will house. They want productions that will have commercial appeal because the more profit the play makes, the more profit the theater makes.

When the musical *Hair* opened in 1968 at the Biltmore, a small, 948-seat house that can accommodate either musicals or straight plays, its producer, Michael Butler, was grateful to get the house. This antiestablishment musical was revolutionary for the commercial theater. It was one of the first Broadway musicals ever produced that minimized plot and maximized an idea, a concept—the concept being a group of hippie kids protesting the Vietnam War and, more subtly, protesting the mores and values of a society that would fight such a war.

It was a show that intentionally made a statement that had the potential for alienating a typical audience. Until recently, the majority of Broadway theatergoers were middle to upper-middle class, middle-aged people—the very group of people mocked and ridiculed in the production.

The question was, of course, would people pay to hear themselves criticized, however entertainingly?

There were other hurdles. Broadway audiences, until then, were accustomed to book musicals, carefully defined works where the music amplified and expanded upon the plot and story line. *Hair* didn't do that. The plot, if it can be called that, is about a young man who is persuaded to burn his draft card in protest at being inducted into the army. To make matters worse, *Hair* featured the legitimate theater's first real on-stage nudity (before *Hair*, the only nudity on Broadway had been above the waist nude females who were not permitted to move, appearing as a set and fixed tableau) and a score that, except for a few tuneful ballads, was strictly rock music.

When the Biltmore owners finally agreed to allow the production to come in, it was on very stiff terms. Of course, the rest is history. *Hair* was the hit of that season, making its investors wealthy. A successful movie sale was made as well.

In 1977, while the film was in production and being shot in various locations around New York, Michael Butler decided that the time was ripe to reopen *Hair*. He did so both to capitalize on the production publicity generated by the film and with the knowledge that revivals of Broadway musicals were suddenly doing pretty good business. He went back to the Biltmore, the site of his past success, and revived the original production of *Hair*, but with a new cast. This time the show was a flop. Its reviews were not good. The idea seemed dated and audiences didn't buy tickets. After a brief run, *Hair* closed.

When choosing a theater, all producers would, ideally, like their production housed in a theater along 44th or 45th Street between Broadway and Eighth Avenue, with 46th

Street a strong second choice. (There are four theaters on 44th Street; six on 45th Street; and four on 46th Street.) This feeling stems from the belief that the more theaters there are close together, the more opportunity there is for last-minute drop-in business—in other words, that if people are coming to see a show in the theater next door and that show is sold out, chances are that they will buy a ticket for your show.

There is also the matter of some of the neighboring streets. Forty-second Street and Eighth Avenue, only a few blocks away, is a center of New York's pornography business and not the safest district, especially at night. Producers feel that many theatergoers may be less reluctant to walk around the Times Square area on streets where theaters are close together, thus increasing the crowds, which, in turn, increases safety.

Both of these are unproven suppositions. If a theater has a popular show, people go anyhow, although they may be a little more watchful on a deserted block with only one theater than they might be on 44th Street. Also, there is not a lot of milling around: theatergoers don't simply decide to go to the theater district and wander from theater to theater to see what show they can get in to. They know in advance where they are going. Nonetheless, to theater people, location is crucial. It is not unheard of for stars to insist upon theater approval in their contract and to keep a play from going into rehearsal until one of these prime-block houses is available.

If one looks to see if there is a pattern of hits or flops according to location, the site does not seem to make any real difference. The Mark Hellinger is relatively far uptown at 51st Street. Yet *My Fair Lady*, at the Hellinger, became the fifth longest running musical in history. Originally an early movie house, the Mark Hellinger was opened in 1930 as the Hollywood Theatre by Warner Brothers, to be a showcase for their films. It became a legitimate house in 1936 with a musical version of *Uncle Tom's Cabin*, and was renamed the Mark Hellinger in 1949 in honor of the Broadway columnist. In addition to *My Fair Lady*, it has housed such productions as *Coco*, starring Katherine Hepburn, and the hit musical, *Sugar Babies*, with Mickey Rooney and Ann Miller.

The Mark Hellinger has one of the most opulent and spacious lobby areas of any Broadway house. Most Broadway theaters do not have large public spaces. It simply doesn't pay. Space—square footage—means money. Real estate owners—in this case, the theater owners—pay taxes on their space. Money is made by having the audience come into the theater to sit and watch the show and not by furnishing additional room in which to congregate between acts or before the show.

Another uptown musical house, the Winter Garden, is located on Broadway between 50th and 51st Streets. It is the original site of the American Horse Exchange (when reviewing a show they didn't like, critics used to claim that they could smell the scent of the old stables) and, with 1,479 seats, is one of the larger musical houses. *West Side Story* began its long run at the Winter Garden in 1957, and Barbra Streisand achieved stardom there in *Funny Girl*. Recently the theater was home to Gilda Radner of "Saturday Night Live" television fame for her limited one-woman engagement, and *42nd Street* opened there in the summer of 1980.

The 1,655-seat Majestic on 44th Street is thought of as the most desirable musical house in New York. It was there that the great Shakespearean actor Sir John Gielgud made his

New York debut. The Richard Rodgers/Oscar Hammerstein classic musicals *Carousel* and *South Pacific* played there, as did *The Music Man* and *Fiddler on the Roof*. Until eclipsed in December 1979 by *Grease*, *Fiddler* was Broadway's longest-running musical. For small dramatic plays, the 781-seat Booth and the 799-seat Golden are considered the most desirable, with the Morosco and the Helen Hayes strong seconds. *The Gin Game* played the Golden and the 1978 Tony Award–winning drama *The Elephant Man* the Booth.

Theater Owners

The relationship between theater owner and producer is unique. Landlords and tenants historically have adversarial relationships, the former trying to maximize the profits, the latter trying to get as many services for the rent as possible. This is true in the theater as well. Certain theaters have the reputation of being well maintained, with good box offices, while others don't. Producers must also consider theater management and service when choosing a house.

However, in the theater there is an additional factor. The more successful the production, the more money the theater owner/landlord stands to make, since theater owners receive a rental fee plus a percentage of the gross box office receipts. If a play is successful, both producer and landlord stand to make money. If the play is a flop or barely limps along, neither makes much money. So in a very real sense the theater owner and the producer are partners.

Negotiating for a theater is the term used when producers book houses for their shows—and negotiate is what they do. It is not simply a matter of going to a theater owner and booking the house. Theater owners are selective about the shows they book, particularly during the busy fall and

The Booth Theater, one of the smallest and most intimate Broadway houses, was built in 1913 by Bostonian Winthrop Ames and named for actor Edwin Booth. It borders on the north end of Shubert Alley, the pedestrian thoroughfare which links 44th and 45th Streets.

Photo by Roger Greenawalt

winter season when more shows open. They too are investing in the property, if only indirectly. Sometimes theater owners help pay advertising costs. Some even insist on the presence of a certain star, director, or other big-name artistic person in the show before they agree to book a production into their theater. Theater owners may agree to cuts in their percentage of the weekly box office receipts just as the artistic people often do—and for the same reason: to give the show an opportunity to build up an audience.

In addition to negotiating the rent and percentage, the

producer also agrees to the figure for the "stop clause." A stop clause stipulates that if the show fails to make an agreed-upon sum of money for two consecutive weeks, (usually a figure under the break-even—the amount of money the production must earn to equal its weekly operating costs), the theater owner can force the show to vacate the house. The show must then close or move to another house.

Theater owners rarely enforce the stop clause unless another production is waiting to enter the theater. A dark house (one in which there is no production) costs money, as taxes and maintenance must be paid; a light house (one in which there is a show) is at least receiving the weekly rent and thus some of the theater's operating expenses. To avoid a dark house, theater owners try to have another show ready to take immediate occupancy when a production closes—close booking is what this is called. Most shows close as a matter of course once it becomes apparent that their audiences are not building and money reserves are disappearing. If their theater is housing an unsuccessful play, theater owners are always on the lookout for another production, one that they hope will be successful and make them money.

In the spring of 1979, at the 22 Steps Theatre, a Broadway middle house, a production called *My Old Friends* was playing. It was not doing well but the producer did not want to close the show, believing it could be resuscitated. However, a one-woman musical, *The Madwoman of Central Park West*, was looking for a theater. Ready to go into production, *The Madwoman of Central Park West* had a reasonable chance of success after receiving good reviews at both its New York off-off-Broadway workshop production and its out-of-town production in Buffalo. It starred Phyllis

Newman, a well-known television and theatrical personality who won a Tony Award for *Subways Are For Sleeping*. When *My Old Friends* failed to make the money agreed upon in the stop clause, the owners of the 22 Steps Theatre forced the producer to close the show in order to allow *Madwoman* to come in. It too failed.

When theater owners are anxious to have a production in their house, they will make concessions to an entering show. *Godspell*, after becoming off-Broadway's third longest running show, moved to Broadway in June 1976. It was booked into the Broadhurst Theatre with the understanding that the production had only to pay the theater's operating expenses through the summer. The Broadhurst had been booked for September by the producers of *A Texas Trilogy*, one of Broadway's most eagerly anticipated productions. Consisting of three full-length plays by Preston Jones, each show repeated every three days. Although the hope was that audiences would want to see all three, each play stood alone and could be viewed as an independent work. The owners of the Broadhurst, the Shubert Organization, did not want their theater dark through the summer and knew that *Godspell* was a good possibility for summer business because it was a family show that would attract New York's summer visitors.

Godspell vacated the Broadhurst in September and moved to the Plymouth, which it then vacated in December to make way for the previously booked *Otherwise Engaged*, a show that went on to win the 1977 New York Drama Critics Circle Award for Best Play. *Godspell* then moved to the Ambassador.

It should be noted that at none of these theaters did *Godspell* make any significant profit. The production usually merely payed expenses. However, it served the purpose of keeping the theaters lit. By keeping open, the show's producers continued to maintain a live and viable production; doing so was very important since they also wanted to create and book road companies to travel throughout the nation.

Sometimes, a Broadway show is booked into a theater as a limited engagement. Occasionally, the show really is going to remain on Broadway or in that theater only for a limited time. The theater may be able to offer a production only an interim booking if its space has been committed to another show for a previously agreed upon date. *Godspell* at the Broadhurst and Plymouth was an interim booking. A star may be available for only a few months or, as with the Richard Burton revival of *Camelot*, out-of-town engagements may have been booked following the New York production.

However, the reality is that most shows advertised as limited engagements are really open-ended engagements. If the production is successful, it is then "extended by popular demand." Billing the show as a limited engagement is especially attractive if the producer does not have funds at his disposal to use in building an audience. It can also be a face-saving device, particularly when a big star is involved. It might be humiliating for a name star to fail on Broadway, which is, of course, what will happen if audiences don't buy tickets. If audiences aren't generated, the show simply closes on the previously announced date.

The Theater Staff

Each Broadway theater employs its own staff of stage hands, electricians, carpenters, propertymen, flymen (the employees who operate the curtain), and box office staff. On a playbill for a Broadway production, after the

biographies of the actors, major artistic people, and producers, there is a listing that says "Staff for the Theater." The names of the major permanent staff of the theater are listed there. The number of permanent employees varies from theater to theater and is a figure negotiated between the theatrical unions and the League of New York Theatres and Producers.

Each theater also has a house manager, who is the day-to-day representative of the theater owner. It is the house manager's responsibility to run the theater and to solve any problems that can affect the audience. He must make sure that the theater is warm enough in the winter and cool enough in the summer. If someone becomes ill during a performance or loses his ticket, the house manager must take care of it. A doctor who thinks he might be called during a performance gives his seat location to the house manager. A good house manager is key to making the audience feel good and receptive to the play. If the audience is uncomfortable, badly treated by ushers or ticket sellers, or otherwise enters with a negative feeling, the pleasure and excitement of the play is spoiled.

Christine Ebersole and Richard Burton starred in a new 1980 production of the Alan Jay Lerner/Frederick Loewe musical *Camelot*. *Camelot* played a limited eight week summer engagement at Lincoln Center's New York State Theater as part of its year long cross-country national tour. *Photo by Martha Swope*

Rehearsal Period:
The Production Comes Alive

When the money has been raised and bonds have been posted with the unions, rehearsal can begin. Rehearsal is the four- to six-week period (usually four for a play and six for a musical), during which all the elements of the production are put together. The goal is, of course, to bring to the stage not only a professional and unified show but a total experience that transcends its parts and becomes theater. In the words of a manager: "It's a little like putting a jigsaw puzzle together. You spread out the pieces, put them together, and hope that they will fit.

"Ideally, everything has come together at the right time. But, you can be sure it hasn't. It so rarely does, especially if you are doing a new production and not one that has had development in another theater.

"Usually, by this time, everyone is going absolutely bonkers. The producer has been infecting everyone with his belief in the show—his enthusiasm, devotion, and commitment—all of which is a way of keeping people on the hook, often for over a year. It's such a balancing act. You've had the director casting the show; the designers at work—all of these people have been working, sometimes getting paid and sometimes not. And, all too often, you never know that definitely that the show will really happen."

The rehearsal period is the point at which the playwright—or if the work is a musical, the lyricist/composer/librettist—hands over control to the director. For a musical this is routine. The work has been a collaborative process from the start. It is a potentially more wrenching time in the case of a play than a musical. For a play, the playwright has written a work and brought the producer a completed script. It reflects a very personal, private statement. The situation is analogous in some ways to a mother giving up her baby for adoption. In an ideal situation, the playwright and director are in agreement about the interpretation and approach to the work, and are personally sympatico. Each has a respect for the other and the ability to work out differences of approach constructively. Many directors and playwrights speak of the relationship that must ensue in terms of a marriage. And as everyone knows, there are problems and disagreements in all marriages, even the best.

It is very rare for the playwright not to have contractual approval of the director selected for his production. Many playwrights have long-standing relationships with certain directors. Edward Albee often works with Alan Schneider, Sam Shepard with Robert Woodruff, Tennessee Williams with Jose Quintero. This issue of interpretation and problem solving which starts between playwright and director and later on in the rehearsal period continues between director and actor is material for a book in itself. Suffice it to say that it is the director who becomes the prominent mover during rehearsal. It is the director's vision as much as the playwright's that shapes the production that will be seen on stage.

Now the various components will be put together on stage by the director. What are they, aside from the obvious ones of how the actors portray the words and ideas encompassed in the script?

Every production—drama, musical, revue, cabaret act—has designers for the set, the costumes, and lighting.

Set Design

The set designer is responsible for the physical scenes—the physical environment—in which the play is seen. One set designer, speaking of her work, says: "Collaboration is the key word. I collaborate with the director and often the playwright as well. I try to discover their feelings about the setting for the work. What I can do as a designer is to translate that feeling into a concrete, visual design."

Sets can range from extremely complex, in which the set itself almost becomes an integral part of the play's action, to a stark backdrop against which the play is performed. They are usually the most expensive part of the production. As often as not, the decision as to whether there will be a single standing set for the entire production or many set changes is based on money. This decision, as everything else in Broadway production, ultimately rests with the producer. Increasingly, only big budget musicals have elaborate and mechanically complicated sets. For small plays, the costs are simply too great.

Set design requires the insight and creativity of an artist and the training of a draftsman and architect. After collaborating with the producer, director, and playwright, the set designer makes a series of rough sketches. This involves historical research if the production is set in a different period of time. Simultaneously with the drawings, the designer is already planning the materials to be used in construction. Once the sketches are approved and accepted, the designer makes a three-dimensional model and draws up design blueprints for the scenic construction crew to use in building a model set.

When the plans for the sets are ready, a bid session is held, usually in the offices of the general manager. It is attended by representatives of the various scenic construction shops. After receiving the relevant information, they prepare bids—prices—for the work. More than economic factors are involved in choosing a shop to build the scenery: some shops have better reputations than others; some producers or set designers have an existing relationship with a particular shop. But usually the shop is chosen as any contractor is for construction work: the one with the lowest bid gets the job.

Costume Design

When costumes are to be made, the costume designer works in a way similar to the set designer: collaboration, sketches, a bid session, and execution. Costumes may be purchased at a department or specialty store, or they may be rented, on a weekly basis, from a costume supply house. It often happens that the same person designs sets and costumes for the show. The costume designer must be an artist who knows and understands fabric, design, color, and how the onstage movements will affect the costume.

The big difference between set and costume design is the personal relationship that exists between actor and costume designer. Costumes are very important to actors. They must feel comfortable in the costume, both physically and emotionally. Sometimes the costume itself becomes the vehicle for what can be called the rite of passage between the actor as individual and the actor as the person portrayed on the stage. Some actors find the very act of dressing—putting on costume, wig, makeup—crucial in making the transition between real life and the stage.

In *Strider*, the actors portrayed peasants in prerevolutionary Russia and also horses. There was no physical set to speak of. A simply hung backdrop and props such as a water trough, a chair, and reins were used to establish scenes. Some scenes called for elaborate period costumes, as when the ensemble portrayed the wealthy gentry of that period. But the other costumes were designed so that the actors could, onstage and in full view of the audience, make the transition back and forth between horse and peasant. They had to create the illusion without change in costume or set.

This was accomplished by using tails. With a flick of the tail—a piece of heavy material with a moplike tassle at the end—the actor could cease being a peasant and portray a horse. This is acting that requires tremendous concentration. Actors must rely totally upon themselves to engage the audience. The audience must believe that at one moment there are people on the stage; at the next, horses.

Some of the tails, for no particular reason, had bushier ends than the others. Each actor became quite attached to his or her own tail. The first time the tails were cleaned, the actors insisted on having their particular tail returned. The tail of Gerald Hiken, the star, was lost. Until it was found a few days later, Hiken felt that an essential tool for his performance was missing. He wanted the tail that had become his.

Lighting Design

Stage lighting can range from the projection of a subtle atmospheric setting to the performance of specific maneuvers within the context of the production. Lighting can make dancers appear to leap higher and farther than they actually do. It can make colors appear different. It can establish time of day and seasons; it can make the same set warm and cozy or menacing and eerie. Lighting can make an actor or actress look beautiful, angry, ugly, or scary.

Theatrical lighting is a highly specialized skill and art. It is different from the lighting for television and movies; in those each scene is individually lit and the action (filming) stopped to allow lights to be changed, added, or removed. In the theater, the entire production must be designed so that the lighting can work with an uninterrupted flow. This means that all the lights must be set and hung in place for the entire production. They must be precisely cued to change with the onstage action as it proceeds.

Sets, lights and costumes are the basics for all productions. If the show is a musical, there is additional personnel exclusive to the musical theater.

Orchestrator: This is the person who takes the composer's music and scores it for the various instruments of the orchestra. The actual musical talents of the composer determine how much the orchestrator must do. For instance, Leonard Bernstein, who composed the music for *West Side Story*, is the former music director of the New York Philharmonic and an eminent composer of classical music. He obviously does not require the same kind of orchestration as a composer who is not musically trained beyond the rudiments of the piano. The orchestrator is often responsible for the musical sound that the audience hears and is analogous to the director who translates the playwright's work to the stage.

Music Director: This is the conductor of the pit orchestra or onstage ensemble. More than a band or orchestra leader, the music director sets the pace for the performance of a musical. This person draws all of the onstage performance elements—dance, song, dialogue—together.

Music Contractor: He or she hires the musicians who play in the theater. Many music directors insist upon acting as their own contractor in order to ensure that the musicians' skills are up to standard and that they are able to work together as a quality ensemble.

Rehearsal Pianists: Just as the name implies, the rehearsal pianists work with the choreographer and music director during dance and vocal rehearsals. Often, the rehearsal pianist assumes the role of vocal coach as well, rehearsing the songs with the principals and chorus members.

Sound Engineer: This is a relatively recent position in the theater. It has arisen as onstage microphones are increasingly used by performers, particularly in musicals. Their work has achieved even greater significance given the growing tendency for performers to lip sync certain numbers, with the actual singing prerecorded. Lip syncing is done when stage movement is so arduous or active that it is impossible—or extremely difficult—for a performer to sing and move at the same time. Liza Minnelli lip synced at least one number during *The Act* and it is said to be done in *A Chorus Line.* Most shows, however, do not happily acknowledge the practice. It has been criticized, as has heavy amplification onstage, which results in an unnaturally loud timbre and tone.

The Stage Manager

Although it is the director who has the overall responsibility for mounting the entire show, in a musical there are often several rehearsals going on at once. The principal dancers and chorus are taught the steps and routines by the choreographer. Vocal coaches and the music director work with the chorus and individual leads. Sometimes, if special dance techniques are necessary, there is a dance specialist who does additional coaching. For instance, if a big number requires tap, a tap-dancing specialist will work with the choreographer and cast. All of this must be coordinated, organized, and scheduled.

At all times, all phases of the show—set and costume construction and lighting boards—must be constantly monitored to make sure that they are adhering to both budget and timetable. Props must be listed and obtained. The day-to-day blocking, the director's actual physical instructions for where the actors stand and move, must be recorded. Script changes, additions, and deletions must be transcribed. The problems that individual actors have, either with one another, the director, or management, must be solved.

The person who coordinates all of this is the stage manager. The stage manager is responsible for everything that happens from the proscenium arch (technically the wall dividing the stage from the audience) to backstage. If the show is to have an out-of-town tryout, the stage manager arranges to ship the scenery to the theater and serves as liaison between the production staff and the theater staff. The job begins during the preproduction period and continues until the show closes, although much of the actual day-to-day work varies, depending upon what phase of production the show is in.

Preproduction: Like many of the people working on the show, stage managers often begin work even before they start receiving a weekly salary, which will not happen until their contract has been signed. This usually takes place when the show goes into rehearsal.

During the preproduction period, stage managers are busy coordinating meetings. They work with the producer, director, and playwright on casting. They usually call agents and casting directors, arrange for audition space, schedule Equity Principal Interviews and chorus calls for dancers and singers. They are present at all auditions and keep track of everyone seen. Record keeping is very important. The director may very well decide, after seeing two hundred people, that he or she liked "that woman with the black hair in the red dress." It is up to the stage manager to know that the woman was number fifty-eight and to arrange immediately for her to be called back and seen again.

Records are also important because they contain the impressions and comments of those who are casting the show. The files will be used often during the show's run to replace cast members who leave, to cast standby positions or parts for a national company that may be formed if the show is a hit. The difference between a standby and an understudy is that a standby is not required to be at the theater unless he or she is actually to perform in place of the actor who is indisposed. The standby must check in before every performance and be available during the show to go on immediately. An understudy plays a supporting role in the show and appears in every performance. Big stars usually have standbys rather than understudies.

Run: It becomes the stage manager's responsibility to maintain the show during its run as the director's representative.

The director usually leaves after the show opens. Often, but not always, directors return periodically to conduct brush-up rehearsals or to direct a replacement who takes over a key role. Basically, though, it is up to the stage manager to keep the show in the shape in which the director leaves it. Stage managers give notes to actors who are deviating in their performance; rehearse understudies at least once a week; rehearse replacements and put them into the show, if the director is unavailable. Sometimes, if the show is so successful that a national company is formed, the stage manager has the authority to cast the parts and direct the production for the road.

During the performance, a stage manager stands at a desk offstage in the wings "calling the show." In front of him is a prompt book, a copy of the script in which every single cue for sound, light, or scene change is recorded. Sometimes a cue will be indicated between two words or even between elongated syllables. A television monitor is mounted above the desk. A closed-circuit television camera located on the front center of the balcony transmits a picture of the onstage proceedings since from the side the stage manager cannot see much of what is happening onstage. He wears a headset with a microphone. Above the desk is a board with a variety of switches and light bulbs linked to similar systems in front of the technicians who man the light, sound, and scenic controls.

Analogous to a controller who works in the control tower of an airport coordinating air traffic, or the person who mans the central computer console of a missile tracking system directing an airborne object in space, the stage manager signals for each light, sound, and scene change that takes place during the performance, including the rise and fall of the curtain.

There are several categories of stage manager. These include the assistant stage manager (ASM), who is often also a chorus member. There is the stage manager. And, there is the production stage manager (PSM). The production stage manager oversees the entire stage and backstage operation and nowadays often receives billing on the title page of the program and the houseboard in front of the theater. The ASM, stage manager, and PSM are all members of Actors' Equity and sign Equity contracts when they are hired.

The fact that stage managers are members of Actors' Equity raises the question of whether the stage manager is management or not. One production stage manager addressing that issue says: "It's a middle position. You have an executive responsibility and you are management in that you are looking out for the producer's interests. You want to make sure he's not spending extra money. For instance, if you don't let the designer know that a certain prop has been cut and it gets built, that's your fault. You are also in charge of everything that happens backstage and must get people to do certain jobs. When the director leaves and you become his representative at the theater, you have to make sure that the performances are kept the way they were directed. You've got to have the respect of the cast and you're definitely in charge then.

"But you're also cast. You're in the actors' union and it's up to you to make sure that management doesn't break any rules like going over rehearsal time. If there's a problem between an actor and management, you become the mediator. You're really a middle man between the producer and the actors. It's not always easy straddling both sides. You've got to be very diplomatic. It's very much a people's job."

In the past few years, a relatively new position has been

created: the production supervisor. This person does not sign an Equity contract, as does a stage manager, but receives a fee and royalty. This puts the position firmly in the category of management. Responsible for opening the show and its maintenance, a production supervisor can work on several productions at once, working full time on a show before opening and then returning periodically, if the director doesn't, for special rehearsals, replacements, and the formation and direction of a national company. Explaining the position, a production supervisor says: "The business has gotten so expensive and compressed into such a short space of time that you need someone who can really grease the way and get things going, especially if the show is a complicated one. The general manager takes care of the individual financial deals and contracts and then I serve as liaison between the creative elements. Somebody has to have clout with everybody on a day-to-day level. But, when the show opens, I replace myself with a production stage manager and come back either at regular intervals to make sure that the show is running the way it's supposed to or when something is happening that requires me."

Press Agent

Outside the rehearsal hall, there is also a lot of activity. The press agent usually goes on contract at this time. The press agent assumes the responsibility for coordinating all the activities that will bring public attention to the show. The groundwork is laid during the rehearsal period so that when the show opens, assuming it runs, an advertising/publicity campaign can start immediately. Sometimes, of course, if there is a big star, a famous playwright or creative team, or the show has been highly successful somewhere else, the show will have a large advance sale. But this is uncommon. Most of the time, a production does not sell that much in advance since most theatergoers wait for the opening and the reviews.

During the rehearsal period, the press agent coordinates the following:

Graphics: This is the logo or picture that will be used in advertisements, on the cover of the program, on posters, window cards (the heavy cardboard posters displayed in windows of ticket agencies, and on the walls of certain restaurants and shops), and the marquee of the theater. It can be a photograph, a sketch, an abstract design, or simply the title of the show set in carefully selected type. Its purpose is to create a readily recognizable image that the public will associate with the show.

Preopening Advertising: Will a full-page ad be taken in the Sunday *New York Times* to announce the play? Or does it make more sense to spend that $19,000 on a half-page ad on Sunday and separate ads on Wednesday and Friday (the two other days considered best for theatrical advertising)? When will the ABC's—the alphabetical listings in daily newspapers of all shows playing on and off Broadway—begin? Should money be spent (if it is available) for radio advertising or for a television commercial before opening?

Front of the House: Outside each theater are glass cases in which pictures, posters, and production photographs appear. The press agent must make sure that the front of the house decorations are completed on time and in accordance with contractual requirements. For instance, contracts with certain principal players may require that photographs be displayed. Unions require a houseboard listing all those who get billing, identical to the title page of the program. Inside the lobby, there is a cast board, which lists every cast member, and an understudy board, which lists the name of any understudy or standby who goes on in place of an actor. There are three ways to announce the appearance of an understudy or standby. Either an announcement is made to the audience immediately before the curtain rises, or inserts are put into the program, or the name of the understudy and the role to be played is posted on the understudy board. Actors' Equity requires that two of these three steps be taken.

The Playbill: This is the program of the play. It is distributed by the ushers as they seat the audience. In Great Britain, there is a charge for programs; in the United States, they are free. Once it is apparent that a musical is a hit and will run, fancy souvenir books are often printed and sold in the lobby, along with other tie-in merchandise such as T-shirts, record albums, and such memorabilia.

The press agent is responsible for all of the production information included in the playbill, although actors, artistic personnel, and producers whose biographies appear must approve them. This is a rule established by theatrical unions and societies. Most biographies are simple paragraphs detailing past acting credits, awards, and training. Some actors may use the space allotted to them to make political appeals or expound on their personal philosophies or beliefs. Some try to be amusing. When appearing in

PLAYBILL

ALVIN THEATRE

Funny Girl, Barbra Streisand included the following in her playbill bio:

> . . . Barbra is a follower of Eastern philosophy and cooking but also favors TV dinners on occasion. She is a renowned collector of antique clothes, shoes and fans. Her favorite flower is the gardenia since it is the only scent that can never be captured. Her favorite day of the week is Tuesday, since she devotes part of each Tuesday throughout the year to stringing crystal beads which are sold in a Vermont general store. She knows how to make coffee ice cream and to fix her own hair. For more personal information, write to her mother.

Since there is only a limited amount of space, often the press agent has the thankless task of restricting the size of an actor's bio. When this happens, most actors are cooperative. However, the egos of some are offended by the restriction to an allotted number of words, and they will use a single line to express their displeasure, as one star did when he offered this bio:

> _____ is still attempting an overnight success after beginning work in the theater at the age of six.

Photo Call: When the set is on stage and costumes are ready, the press agent sets the time for a photo call. This photo session takes place onstage, at the theater. A limited amount of time is available for a photo call. If it goes over that time, the producer has to start paying overtime. Hence, the

The playbill from *Annie.*

photographer must be highly skilled, shooting in both color and black and white and in the time allowed. The photographs will be used for the cases in front of the house, with reviews, when they are published, and in newspapers and magazines. This is part of the publicity and advertising campaign. Newspapers and magazines are very selective about what they publish. A good, exciting photograph has a much greater chance of being used than a dull or amateurish one.

Out-of-Town Tryouts

At the completion of rehearsal, all the actors know their lines. They know where and how to move on the stage. They work together as an ensemble, feeding off one another and reacting to the events onstage as participants. However, they are performing in a vacuum. A crucial element is missing—the audience. There can be no theater without one. Ultimately, the best playwright, director, or actor cannot know what really works onstage and what doesn't until there is an audience. Edward Albee, referring to the actors in his plays, once said in a *New York Times* interview, "Sometimes, they'll come offstage after their first performance of the work in front of an audience and they'll grab me, look at me with wild eyes and say, 'Edward, this play is funny.' "

Before the show is performed in front of an audience, there is no way of knowing whether or not the lines will get laughs, whether a moment intended to be moving will be so and not mawkishly sentimental, whether a certain piece of staging is effective.

Performing the show in front of an audience is the final stage of the rehearsal period. It is often a time when major changes are made—new songs added, sets changed, characters dropped, script revised or rewritten, even actors replaced. Traditionally, shows used to go out of town at this point. There, in cities such as New Haven or Atlantic City, extensive revisions and reworking could be done. Writers would work out of hotel rooms and composers and lyricists would write music and lyrics for new material literally overnight. Often a production would spend weeks out of town, developing and refining the show until it was ready for Broadway.

Today, fewer and fewer productions go out of town for a pre-Broadway tryout. Most producers cannot afford it. Besides, most plays have had development in regional or off-off-Broadway theater before coming to Broadway. This has replaced the out-of-town tryout for plays. However, musicals, especially those that have not had a workshop, regional, or off-off-Broadway production, do profit from out-of-town tryouts. One producer says: "You really should go away to make your mistakes. Once you open your doors in New York, the word is out. If you're out of town and people are talking about you, saying, 'What do you hear about _____?' and someone answers 'They're in a lot of trouble,' the reaction is just not the same as if you're in New York. It just doesn't matter the same way. Out of town, you're expected to be working on the show and what people say just doesn't have the impact it does when you're in New York."

Nowadays, a show usually has a tryout in Boston, Philadelphia, or Washington, D.C. However, since most shows are reviewed out of town and these are major cities, a producer will often try to open first for a brief run in a smaller city, such as Wilmington, Delaware. Although the show business trade publication, *Variety*, prints reviews, bad out-of-town reviews in the local press, while they do not influence New York theatergoers, can start negative talk in the trade. This can affect advance booking of theater parties and groups.

Nevertheless, since out-of-town is a place where shows are expected to be changed, the trade expects a show to come to New York in a substantially different form. *Fiddler on the Roof* had an entire new musical number added four days before its New York engagement. *Annie*, which originated at Connecticut's Goodspeed Opera House and then went on to Washington's John F. Kennedy Center for the Performing Arts, went through numerous changes, including the replacement of the original Annie with Andrea McCardle, who went on to achieve fame in the role.

Funny Girl, which brought Barbra Streisand national fame, spent weeks working out its problems. The show first had Jerome Robbins as its director. Mr. Robbins is one of the musical stage's and classical ballet's foremost director/choreographers. He conceived, directed, and choreographed *West Side Story* and directed *Fiddler on the Roof*. However, he left *Funny Girl* after a dispute about the book. Bob Fosse came on next, although he also quit the production. Garson Kanin then took over the direction through *Funny Girl*'s Boston and Philadelphia tryouts. When the show opened in Boston, it was much too long and there were problems with many of the songs. Thirty minutes were cut from the production.

In Philadelphia, there were still book and musical problems and an additional thirty minutes were cut. Even when the show came to New York, more than an hour shorter than it had been and with the deletion of five songs, there were still problems and the opening was postponed five times. In order not to displace Kanin, Robbins was asked to return as production supervisor. However, this prompted Kanin's resignation. When the show finally opened in 1964, it was a success. But, without those many weeks on the road and in preview in New York, *Funny Girl* would most likely have been a disaster.

The theater is full of productions that hardly anyone has heard of which closed out of town before coming to New York. They represent substantial financial losses to producers and investors. Some featured many of the theater's biggest stars, including Yul Brynner in *Home Sweet Homer*, Della Reese in *The Last Minstrel Show*, Jerry Lewis in *Hellzapoppin*, and Carol Channing in *The Bed Before Yesterday*.

Often, when a show is in trouble out of town, consultants are brought in to work on it. They are called play doctors and are just what the word implies: directors who are asked to come in, diagnose the problem, and make the play well. This is a delicate business. When a show is in trouble, its director is under tremendous pressure. His position becomes precarious when the producer calls in a doctor. The suggested therapy may include replacing the director. When a play doctor is called in, the director often feels he is losing credibility with the cast. Everybody's state of mind becomes more tense. Many times, a producer will ask a play doctor to sneak in to see the production. Arriving out of town from New York, the doctor/director hopes not to be recognized as he slips into the theater, usually sitting far in the rear. It is only after private conversation with the doctor that the producer decides whether to replace the current director or incorporate some of the doctor/director's suggestions into the production.

Preview Performances

Whether or not a show does have an out-of-town tryout, it always has preview performances in New York. These are

performances to which critics and press are not invited—
nor are they even allowed to attend unless specifically invited by the producer through the press agent. The director
is often still rehearsing the cast during the day, adding and
deleting material. Preview tickets used to be priced lower
than those for regular performances, but this is rarely true
today. However, previews are when the real New York
word of mouth starts on a show. Within the theatrical community, everyone always knows what show is opening and
on what evening. Many see the show in preview and there is
usually a lot of talk about the play. Often, by the time
opening night comes, there are no surprises.

8

Opening Night:
The Audience, the Critics,
the Reviews

I t is finally opening night! Years of planning, months of
work, and hundreds of thousands of dollars—perhaps
millions—are at stake—not to mention the hopes of
everyone associated with the show. At every level, there is
excitement and anticipation. For the investors, there is the
chance to be the proud supporters of a hit and the opportunity to make a lot of money. For the artistic people and
the actors, there is the hope of receiving the kind of notices
and reviews that mean future employment and success. A
failure means, in many cases, a trip to the unemployment
lines. A hit means work.

For everyone, however, the money and the job are only
secondary. Most people work in the theater because they
love it. Henry Fonda spoke of this in 1978 in an interview before the opening of *First Monday in October*, in which he
played a Supreme Court Justice; "I feel I'm indulging
myself when I come back to the theater. I'm not doing it for
your benefit or for the audience's benefit. It's for me. I am
having the most fun in my life. It's what I love."

Broadway openings are gala, star-studded events, unique
to the entertainment business. It used to be common for

movies also to have large openings. Klieg lights were set up outside the theater and stars arrived in limousines. This is increasingly rare as the big movies now open simultaneously in different cities throughout the land. Fanfare is usually limited to advertising and publicity. With a Broadway show, it is different. There is one single production and thus, one single place—one theater—on which to focus. It is live. The special magic associated with the theater is intact.

Traditionally, openings are black tie, with men in tuxedos and women in formal gowns, although over the years even Broadway openings have become less formal occasions. The opening night audience is mostly an invited one. It consists of the show's backers, who are given the opportunity to come to this glamorous event—but must purchase their seats; celebrities who want to be seen and photographed; friends and fans of the cast and producer; and the drama press and critics, whose collective judgment will decide the fate of the show.

Telegrams, flowers, and messages pour into the theater and are delivered to the dressing rooms. Theatrical superstitions and traditions abound on opening nights. It has been known for an opening night date to be chosen after the producer consults with an astrologer. One Tony Award–winning actress will sign contracts only on auspicious dates, also after seeing her astrologer. A bad dress rehearsal is a harbinger of success, and rain on opening night is considered good luck. "Break a leg!" is the traditional good luck line given to actors. This expression comes from the superstition that one shouldn't tempt the gods by asking for luck and success because the gods have the habit of doing the opposite of what they are asked to do. The French whisper a swear word, *"Merde."* All these superstitions

arise from the basic human need to try to control what cannot be controlled, especially in times of stress. And openings
are times of stress.

Many actresses and actors have certain amulets or good
luck charms they wear on their bodies or keep in their dressing rooms. Certain rituals often become necessary for an actor to feel secure before going out on stage. Sometimes, just
before the curtain goes up, the entire cast meets on stage for
a moment of silent thought on the performance. They use
this time as an opportunity to confirm and reinforce the
communal effort of their production, and also to transfer
themselves from the real world to that of the fantasy of the
stage. The cast of *Fiddler on the Roof* had such a ritual
before each performance, and the cast of an off-Broadway
show called *Piano Bar* gathered on stage just before the
doors were opened for the audience and sang the hymn
"Amazing Grace."

The opening night curtain is scheduled for 6:30 P.M. instead of the usual 8:00 P.M. curtain time. This allows critics
to write or broadcast their reviews in time for the late news
or morning newspapers. The curtain is held, though, until
6:45 P.M. in order to allow critics to arrive at the last
minute. It is rare for critics to mingle with the opening
night audience. They are there to work, not to socialize.
They are usually very careful to avoid any comment that
might publicly forecast their review.

Following the opening, there is usually an opening night
party. It is usually held in one of the theatrical restaurants
near the theater. Sardi's has, traditionally, been the site of
more opening night parties than any other restaurant.

In the entrance to Sardi's, on 44th Street, are posters of
current Broadway and off-Broadway productions. The
posters are constantly being moved around so that current

plays meet the eye first. Along the restaurant's walls are caricatures of stars. It is an honor, a mark of arrival, for a star to have his or her caricature up on the wall, especially along the left bank of tables, which, for some reason, has become the most prestigious seating area in the restaurant.

A Broadway fixture for many years, Sardi's is operated by Vincent Sardi. He has extended credit to many actors during lean times, knowing they would pay their bills when they got work. Sardi's has a special "actors' menu," with reduced prices, and its bar is always crowded with theatrical people before and after showtime. In the upstairs Belasco Room, the site of numerous backers' auditions, opening night parties, theater awards parties and presentations, even theatrical union chapter meetings are often held.

After the play, the opening night guests arrive talking, waiting at the bar for drinks, and lining up at the buffet. As the stars and other cast members arrive, they are applauded. Around 10:30 P.M., the first reviews come in. By 11:30, when the television reviews have been broadcast, everyone knows whether the show is a hit or a flop, or as is often the case, a bit of both. The producer must now decide whether to close or make a run for it. This decision is usually determined by how much money remains for advertising and promotion and for meeting the production's weekly operating expenses.

In his autobiography, *Musical Stages*, the late Richard Rodgers describes the triumphant reception received by his and Oscar Hammerstein's first collaboration, *Oklahoma!* The day after the opening, both of them went to the theater to look at the lines forming at the box office. A theatrical dream had come true. The crowds were so great that a policeman had been called in to keep order. Rodgers writes:

Since Oscar and I had made an appointment for lunch, I asked him, "Shall we sneak off to someplace quiet where we can talk, or shall we go to Sardi's and show off?" "Hell, let's go to Sardi's and show off," said Oscar, and we did. From the moment we walked in until we left, everyone kept crowding around us congratulating us, hugging us, kissing us, telling us they were on their way to buy tickets—or asking us to try to get them some—all the while assuring us that they had known from the start that the show would be a hit.

However, all too often opening night involves the following tale told by a young actress who had a featured role in a Broadway musical which opened and closed in one night. Describing the opening night party, she said:

We felt we had done a good job and the show had gone well. After the curtain came down, we ran backstage and all the producers were there. Our faces were flushed and we were all jumping up and down and hugging each other. We really thought it had been good.

We went to the party. It was at Sardi's and I went downstairs with my parents first and we celebrated and felt great. I should have left it at that. I shouldn't have gone upstairs to the party. It was crowded and hot and I couldn't get into conversation with anyone. It turned out not to be good but we were all still feeling terrific about the show and did think we were going to get good reviews. We were saying things like, "Oh, it will run six months, at least."

And then, after I'd been at the party for about an hour and a half, the air—I don't know how I knew because there wasn't anything that physically you could see or point to that happened but I knew the reviews were out and that they were bad.

I looked and saw one of the producer's sons standing there with an expression that could kill. I walked over and said, "You've heard the reviews." And he said, "Yes, it's just starting to filter through." I said, "Well, what?" He said, "We died . . . we're dead"; and then I remember him saying, "But you made out all right . . . but we're dead."

And then it just happened like that . . . like a forest fire. It just took off through the room. All conversation stopped and groups started the huddle. _____ [the star], I saw her in tears in the corner with the producer's arm around her. It was just like somebody had died.

The worst part was that they just weren't fair. The critics were much meaner than they should have been. Within fifteen minutes, that place was empty.

—So goes opening night.

The Opening Date

The opening date is set by registering with the League of New York Theatres and Producers or, in the case of an off-Broadway production, the League of Off-Broadway Theatres. If the show is a Broadway production, no other Broadway show will open on that date. This is because the first-night critics cannot attend two shows at once. Off-Broadway and off-off-Broadway are different. It is not uncommon, especially during the busy mid-October weeks when the fall season is getting under way, for a Broadway, off-Broadway, and several off-off-Broadway productions to open on the same night.

Sometimes shows postpone their opening if the producer and director feel that more time is needed to get the production into better shape. Some shows never open or at least attempt to avoid a formal opening, not wanting to risk the possibility of bad reviews. This occurs more frequently off- and off-off-Broadway, especially when producers intend to work on the show, raise money, and hopefully move the production to Broadway. A show may be only in development or in workshop form. Producers don't want to alienate potential investors with negative reviews of a work in progress.

Broadway shows, however, usually do open on the date set. It is difficult to build an audience without reviews, and it is a rare producer who has the funds to keep a production running in preview indefinitely. In any case, critics will usually make sure the Broadway production opens. When *Sarava*, a 1979 musical based on the film *Dona Flor and Her Two Husbands*, postponed its opening date twice, critics, led by *The New York Times*'s, suspected that its producers had decided not to open and to take their chances by running indefinitely in preview. Most critics purchased their own seats and reviewed *Sarava*. They did not find much to support and the show closed shortly thereafter. That same season, when *I Remember Mama* postponed its opening for the second time, its producer informed *The New York Times* that he did, indeed, intend to open the show and requested that they not review it until the newly set—third—opening date.

Traditionally, the fall has been Broadway's most active time. Years ago, the commercial theater was relatively inactive during the summer with only holdover hits from past seasons continuing during the hot months. It was rare for new productions to open in the late spring or summer. Today though, Broadway flourishes throughout the year and it is no longer so uncommon for new productions to open in the spring.

As a matter of fact, certain productions seem to benefit from a late season opening. Under the best of circumstances, dramas have more trouble generating audiences than musicals or comedies. Whereas a musical or comedy can overcome mixed reviews and notices, it is almost impossible for a dramatic production to do this. Some of Broadway's biggest hits of the past few years, including *The Wiz*, *The Best Little Whorehouse in Texas*, *Grease*, and *Chapter Two* received mixed notices. They were all musicals and comedies. Even dramatic productions that receive overwhelmingly favorable reviews have a difficult time building audiences.

The Elephant Man won the 1978 Tony Award for best play. It had moved to Broadway that spring after a successful off-off-Broadway production. However, there were many who believed that *The Elephant Man* would not have succeeded if it had not won the Tony within a few weeks of its Broadway opening. The Tony Awards ceremonies are televised nationally to an audience in the millions. The excitement and publicity generated by the awards caused *The Elephant Man* to become a "hot ticket" with sold-out houses.

Another drama, *Wings*, had opened in the fall. Written by Arthur Kopit, whose play *Oh Dad Poor Dad, Mama's Hung You in the Closet and I'm Feeling So Sad* is frequently performed in regional theaters, *Wings* received almost unanimously favorable reviews. Starring Constance Cummings, *Wings* was nominated for a Tony for best play and the Tony for best actress in a play was shared, in an unprecedented move, by Miss Cummings and Carole Shelley, star of *The Elephant Man*. Yet when the Tonys were presented in early June, *Wings* had been closed for months. A serious drama, the production had opened early in the season and had been unable to attract sufficient audience to remain open.

Since it is so difficult to build audiences for serious plays and awards do seem to make a difference, there is talk these days among producers and knowledgeable theater people that it probably makes more sense to open dramas toward the end of the season, since the various theatrical awards are announced in late spring. If a show opens in early spring, in time to be nominated and considered for the major theatrical awards and wins, its producers can cash in on the audience-building power of the awards.

The Opening-Night Audience

Once the opening is set, critics and press are informed and invited. Each fall, the League of New York Theatres and Producers publishes two lists: the first-night list and the second-night list. Comprised of critics, drama editors and writers on newspapers and magazines, radio and television talk-show hosts and producers, and syndicated columnists such as Liz Smith and Earl Wilson whose columns appear in newspapers throughout the nation, the first- and second-night lists are a "suggested" guide to the distribution of press (complimentary) seats.

On the first-night list are "first-string" critics, those who review for major newspapers and magazines, the wire services (Associated Press and United Press International), and the major television and radio stations. Second night is for second-string critics. Second night is not necessarily the night following opening. A show can open on Sunday, be dark on Monday, and have its second night on Tuesday. The revival of *Peter Pan* starring Sandy Duncan, the first musical to open the 1979–80 season, opened on a Thursday and then had its second nights for three evenings the following week. Of course, if a play closes after opening night, there is no second night.

Sometimes, if a show receives bad first-night reviews, many of the second-night critics and editors don't bother to come, thinking that the show may not be around when their publications print the review. However, this is really not fair, as award-winning performances can be given in terrible shows and the second-night press votes on many of the theatrical awards ballots. Not to attend a production is irresponsible, and there are some press agents who remove a person from the second-night list if he or she doesn't show up.

Each Broadway house has a seating chart indicating the exact number and location of each seat. Using this chart as a guide, the press agent assigns seats to the invited press. This is easier said than done as people are often very conscious of where they are placed in comparison to others. It is important not to slight one critic over another by assigning a less desirable seat. Representatives of comparable publications and radio/television stations are usually given identical locations. For instance, the critics from *Time* and *Newsweek* are usually placed in aisle seats on opposite ends of the same row. The *New York Times* critic, the most influential and important reviewer, is in the best seats but comparable seats are given to the critics on the other two New York City daily newspapers, the *New York Post* and the *Daily News*. Associated Press and United Press International, the wire services that send reviews and stories to newspapers throughout the nation, receive seats in much the same fashion as *Time* and *Newsweek* critics.

Almost as important as where the critics sit are the locations given to key drama editors and radio/television producers. The press agent doesn't want to offend them as they, more than likely, will be asked to help publicize the show by having the stars and cast members make appearances and give interviews.

As mentioned before, the first- and second-night lists

merely "suggest" those who may be invited to openings. Although it is virtually unheard of for a critic or writer on the first- or second-night list not to be invited because of past reviews, it has happened. In 1915, the Shuberts produced *Taking Chances*. It opened to uniformly bad notices, including one from the *New York Times* critic, Alexander Woollcott.

When the Shuberts read the Woollcott review, they were so angry that they barred Woollcott from all of their theaters. Woollcott immediately sued to prevent the Shuberts from carrying this out. He won. However, the Shuberts appealed the ruling and the case went to the court of appeals. There the lower court decision was reversed; the court stated that since a theater is private property, its owners could decide whom they wanted to seat or bar as long as they did not exclude on the basis of race or religion.

The entire affair, however, became a national issue, with public opinion very much against the Shubert position. The Shuberts, led by Lee Shubert, eventually backed down and informed *The New York Times* that Woollcott would be welcome to attend productions in their theaters.

More recently, John Simon, the critic for *New York Magazine*, was temporarily removed from the first-night list after his review of Liza Minnelli when she opened in *The Act*. Basing much of his review on a vitriolic and highly unflattering description of her physical attributes, it was one of a series of notices he had written in which he seemed to review not the play or acting as much as the physical and psychological characteristics of its star. The League of New York Theatres and Producers decided that Simon should be censured for what they, and most others, considered to be irresponsible and destructive criticism. Although most producers continued to instruct their press agents to invite

Simon to their openings, the point was publicly made when the League, on behalf of the theatrical community, made it quite clear that one of its criteria for inclusion on the first- and second-night lists was responsible criticism and not gratuitous attack.

Critics and Reviews

In the winter of 1980, the League of New York Theatres and Producers compiled statistics to show the impact of reviews on potential theater audiences. As reported in *Variety*, the five local television stations that review the Broadway theater have a combined viewing audience of 4 million. The three New York City daily newspapers have a combined readership of about 3 million.

What is interesting, of course, is what these figures mean to Broadway. Although New York television has the largest audience of potential theatergoers—a million more than the three city dailies combined—the general feeling is that television reviews do not have the impact of newspapers, especially of *The New York Times*. If a show receives good television notices but a bad *Times* review, sometimes a producer will use the TV quotes in hopes that the show can be saved. However, the consensus is that good television notices alone cannot make for a successful run. What does seem to be true, however, is the reverse. Uniformly bad television notices can doom a show even if many of the print reviews are favorable.

Producers and those who work in the theater have been increasingly concerned about television critics. The medium itself exists primarily to entertain. The nightly half-hour news broadcasts devote more time to the weather and sports than they do to a Broadway play or musical. The seventy to eighty seconds available for review often exclude serious thought. And the pressures to be entertaining some-times result in flippant reviews. To dismiss a serious effort in a humorous, put-down manner can be both devastating and unfair. At least those who publish their reviews in print must think through and develop their positions about a production.

The New York Times has, however, over the years come under the harshest criticism from producers who know that the *Times* has the power to make or break a show. The prestige of the *Times* is such that its review is inevitably the most important one a show can get. This has always been so. It is even more so today as there are only three daily newspapers in New York City, a far cry from 1914 when there were thirteen dailies and twenty years ago when there were six. A rave from the *Times* can mean a sellout au-dience, while a bad review can doom a show even when there are other favorable notices.

Even recently the *Times* was publicly attacked by as prominent a theater luminary as Neil Simon. When his show *They're Playing Our Song* opened to uniformly good notices except from the *Times*, Simon was quoted in *Variety* as saying:

> I watched Richard Eder [the *Times* critic] reviewing a show once. I sat up in the box and watched him. The curtain went up, he looked at the stage for about 10 seconds, and then literally wrote for about 10 minutes. Then he looked up again, but by now the actors were not where he was looking, so he looked over there and he watched and then he was writing again for another 10 minutes. He should be reviewing radio.

As it happened, Richard Eder was replaced as the major *New York Times* critic in the fall of 1979 by Walter Kerr.

Kerr had held the post previously, leaving to write a weekly theater column for the Sunday *New York Times*. When Kerr returned to daily criticism, he hoped to avoid last-minute deadlines and attended final preview performances in advance of opening night. This prompted criticism from theater people, who were unhappy that Kerr's reviews appeared in the *Time's* first edition at about 10:00 P.M., in advance of the television reviews. When Kerr resigned in the fall of 1980 to resume the weekly column, Frank Rich was appointed first-string critic at the *Times*. A relatively unknown quantity as a reviewer to most in the theater, Frank Rich, only in his early thirties, became in 1980 the most important critic on Broadway.

Basically, the theater critic is in an awkward position because no one in the theater likes the function of the critic. There is even a saying that "the only good critic is a dead or retired one."

The critics, of course, feel differently. They want productions to be successful and to run. Yet the very word "critic" means to make a judgment—to find fault. Critics are not in the easiest of positions, especially when reviewing off-off-Broadway and certain off-Broadway productions. These often involve artistic and creative risk and in fairness should not be judged by the same criteria as commercial Broadway productions. While some critics are educated in the theater and have a dramatic background and understanding, most perceive themselves as representing an audience that is paying a large sum of money to be entertained.

As one critic for a large chain of newspapers said: "I think it is important for critics to be journalists first as opposed to theater people. I am suspicious of critics who are frustrated actors, directors or playwrights who really want to be in the theater and use the job of critic as the way to stay in it. I have a journalistic mission, which is to report.

"If I side with anyone, I side with the paying audience. I am paid to sit in for the audience. That's my point of view. It might sound terrible to say this but in some ways you should be ignorant to give a knowledgeable assessment. My best background is my experience as a full-time theatergoer seeing plays almost every night. I do think, however, that the specific instances dictate. If I am reviewing a classic—a Shakespeare production, for instance—I make sure I know the play. I often read it again. Because when you review a classic, you are reviewing the production, not the play itself."

Although it sounds like a glamorous job—what could be better than attending Broadway openings, especially for free?—it has its pitfalls. Each year, about fifty productions open on Broadway. Perhaps three times that number open off-Broadway, and approximately six hundred productions are produced off-off-Broadway each season, of which about eighty are by the major off-off-Broadway companies. As mentioned, at certain times there are a greater number of openings. For the month of October 1980, the Theatre Information Bulletin listed over twenty-five productions, and it does not list every single off-off-Broadway opening.

Theater critics review each Broadway opening and almost every off-Broadway opening. Most try, as well, to cover the major off-off-Broadway offerings by such established companies as the New York Shakespeare Festival, Manhattan Theatre Club, Playwrights Horizons, and several others. Whenever they can, critics will attend additional off-off-Broadway productions, even when they know that they will not have the newspaper space to do a review.

In addition, most critics also write about theater and interview theatrical personalities, playwrights, and directors. As the critic quoted above went on to say: "There simply isn't time to do everything. I get so much mail it's indescribable. When I was away last August, there were two bags waiting for me. I don't have a secretary and I get literally thousands of press releases, invitations to openings, and letters requesting I interview a certain person. The other week, I was up almost around the clock. I had two Sunday pieces to do, an advance piece on a big musical that was opening that week, and an interview. I also had to keep up with my daily reviewing, which involves seeing anywhere from three to eight shows a week for eleven months a year or even twelve, if I don't take a vacation."

Unlike some of the television and radio critics who also review film and television and must condense their reviews into time slots of about two and a half minutes maximum, those who work for newspapers and many of the magazines review only the theater. And most feel, as this critic says, that "Broadway is the source . . . the prize . . . the real diamond."

After the Reviews

If most of the reviews are raves, the play is a hit and everyone is deliriously happy. Years of work have culminated in good notices and there is no feeling to match it. Everyone can settle down for a long and successful run, and a regular salary.

If the reviews are negative, the show often closes on opening night or the week following. A producer who anticipates bad reviews and is willing and psychologically able to acknowledge that the show is, indeed, in trouble will often post a closing notice before opening. The closing notice is a brief announcement stating that the show will close on a specified date. It is a union requirement that the notice be posted a week in advance of closing.

When a notice is posted, the cast and all personnel associated with the production are freed from the contractual commitment to remain with the show and can leave. However, sometimes a show finds a "break-even" audience. In such a case, the show runs for weeks with a closing notice posted. Each week that the show runs, the notice is removed and a new one, announcing a closing date for the following week, is posted. This kind of uncertainty can be hellish on the cast and it is certainly not a happy or relaxed time for anyone.

But what happens when the reviews are mixed? Some critics may have liked the production. They may have reacted favorably to certain aspects of the show or certain performances. In that case, producers have something with which to work in building an audience and usually decide to run the show. They will now begin to promote the production—to inform the public about it in such a positive way that they will want to buy tickets.

Promoting the Show: Advertising and Publicity

When a production has opened and its producers feel that there is a reasonably good chance of building an audience, the marketing of the show begins immediately. There are two aspects to promoting or marketing a Broadway production: advertising and publicity. The difference between the two is simple. Advertising is purchased. Publicity is free.

Only four advertising agencies specialize in theater. The advertising agency buys ad space from newspapers and magazines and commercial time from radio and television stations. Print advertising is sold by the line; radio and television time is sold by the minute or second.

A *New York Times* advertisement may be 180 on two: an ad of 180 lines (the vertical measurement) running horizontally over two column spaces (newspapers are always divided into columns). Such an ad would come out to an advertisement measuring approximately 13″ long and 4″ wide. In television and radio, advertising representatives speak of a "buy," which entails either sixty-second spots, thirty-second spots, or ten-second spots, although ten-second spots are rarely used.

In newspapers and magazines, publicity is any mention

of the show in the editorial pages: a feature story, a photograph of a celebrity going backstage after seeing the production, an interview with one of the stars, or even mention in a gossip column. On television or radio, publicity can be an appearance on a feature segment of the nightly news broadcast, a guest appearance on an interview show or on a panel discussion, or even an appearance by one of the stars or cast members on a local game show. All this is free. No one pays for that time or space. Let's talk about advertising first.

Television

In the last few years, theatrical advertising has changed radically because of television. Indeed, the use of television as an advertising medium has changed the Broadway theater. For the sake of convenience, let's place theatergoers in one of two categories: the regular theatergoers and the general public. Some people attend the theater regularly. They are interested in theater and attend theatrical productions routinely. This audience goes to dramatic productions as well as musicals and comedies. The general public rarely goes to the theater or goes only a couple of times a year. They tend to see musicals and successful comedies. They are reached through television advertising.

The first show to advertise over television was a musical called *Pippin*. Produced in 1973, it was the story of Pippin, the son of the ninth-century emperor of the Holy Roman Empire, Charlemagne. In an advertisement that is now a classic and one of the best ads ever produced, one minute of dancing from *Pippin* was shown over television. The ad concluded by telling the television audience that if they enjoyed this one minute from *Pippin*, they should come to the theater and see the other 119 minutes of the show. Many people who work in the theater say that the one minute from *Pippin* shown on television was the best thing about the show. But the point is the commercial worked. *Pippin* had opened to mixed reviews but became a huge financial success, running for over three years and generating profits in the millions.

Following on the heels of *Pippin* and establishing television as a viable and essential advertising medium for a musical was *The Wiz*, a black version of *The Wizard of Oz*. When *The Wiz* opened on Broadway, it did not receive very good reviews. The first week after its opening, *The Wiz* grossed only about $53,000, far from its $70,000 break-even figure. Box office revenues gradually increased, but the show did not have the makings of a hit. Ticket buying was on a performance-by-performance basis. Such a buying pattern is an indication that the audience consists of the regular theatergoers, whereas an advance sale shows that the general public, which plans theatrical attendance as a special event, is buying.

Ken Harper, *The Wiz*'s producer, decided to make a television commercial. One of the show's best numbers, a song that became a national hit, "Ease On down the Road," was used. The week after the television commercial started to appear, the box office receipts jumped to about $100,000 per week and the show started playing to standing-room audiences. *The Wiz* began building a box office advance and soon became a hot ticket. The success of television for *The Wiz* and *Pippin* opened up an entirely new medium for the promotion of Broadway shows. Television advertising has also been responsible for the increasingly longer runs of many Broadway musicals and comedies. *Grease*, at this writing Broadway's longest-running musical, is a case in point.

Today, one knowledgeable advertising executive talks about the necessity of television advertising for a musical: "It is a terrible mistake for any show to budget itself just through opening night. Usually, a musical will budget $50,000 for the production of a television commercial to be in the can and ready to run immediately after opening. However, when the sets start costing more than was planned or the costumes double in cost, the producers take the television money and spend it just to get the show open. If I could give anyone advice, I would say that if you can raise $1 million for a musical, you should raise $1,300,000. You should make the commercial in advance and start airing it the minute the show opens."

Television is very expensive. It costs between $30,000 and $50,000 just to make a sixty-second commercial. Buying time on television to air the commercial costs about $25,000 a week. All television commercials should be aired for at least three to five weeks. A common belief among advertising people is that no commercial has been seen unless it has been seen at least three times. It seems to take that much exposure for the message to sink in.

In advertising terminology, television is considered a direct impulse buy. When a television (or radio, for that matter) commercial is aired, the telephone number for Chargit is always printed below and announced. The hope is that viewers will rush to the phone and call Chargit to reserve seats. It is not ordinarily a good idea to air a television or radio commercial before the show has actually opened or is at least in preview. As one advertising expert says: "You don't buy television time and air a commercial for an event that is happening next month."

Unlike most forms of advertising, television does have a measurable effect. There is a science to it. One advertising executive says: "If you run a television commercial, you can see its effect. The box office should go up fifty percent within the next week. When the national company of *They're Playing Our Song* opened in Chicago, the first week it played to half capacity. Then, they started to air the television commercial. The next week, the show sold out."

Television is not used only to spark interest in a show that may be in trouble. When *Annie* and *A Chorus Line* opened, both were instantaneous hits. Yet both ran television commercials immediately after opening to build up future sales. When a substantial advance had been built, both shows stopped television advertising, resuming it periodically when they wanted to build their advance again and remind their audiences that they were still on Broadway. Such television commercials are establishment commercials— they establish the production, imprinting its name and hit status on people's minds.

Sometimes a show creates its own magic even before opening as did *Golda*, discussed in the second chapter. In 1979, the musical *Evita* generated a magic. Advertising and promotion do not make the magic, but they do reinforce and capitalize on it. *Evita* had all the makings of building that kind of preopening mystique. It had been a sellout in London. It was produced and directed by Harold Prince, whose production of *Sweeney Todd* had won eight Tony Awards the season before. Its subject matter was fascinating—the rise to power and subsequent death of the young and beautiful wife of the Argentinian fascist dictator Juan Perón. *Evita* was a rags-to-riches story of an ambitious poor girl. Eva Perón, a woman with tremendous charisma, managed to gain the support of an entire nation while amassing great personal wealth. She also suppressed and jailed those who threatened her power and that of her hus-

Wednesday matinee crowds gather in front of the 1788 seat Broadway Theater to attend a performance of the 1979-80 season's biggest musical hit, *Evita*. Based on the life of Eva Perón, *Evita* came to Broadway from London where it continued to remain one of the most popular theatrical attractions in Great Britain's history.

Photo by Roger Greenawalt

band. It was a chilling story and, at the same time, glamorous. One of the show's songs, "Don't Cry for Me, Argentina," was widely played over radio stations throughout the country even before the show opened.

The preproduction advertising campaign capitalized on this excitement. New York City buses carried big signs heralding the coming of *Evita*. A large billboard was rented on Broadway and the *Evita* logo displayed. Newspapers and magazines carried stories about the opening, something that does not usually happen except for a big and eagerly awaited production. Even negative publicity didn't seem to hurt the advance buildup; it only fascinated people more. Several writers found the idea of the show offensive: they felt that *Evita* glorified one of the most evil and destructive women in history. When *Evita* did open, this feeling permeated some of the reviews and they were not the raves that had been anticipated and hoped for. However, word of mouth and excitement had built up. *Evita* had become an event. It was a play that people felt they had to see and were willing to plan months ahead in order to see. And even after a year and a half, the production continued to play to sell-out audiences.

While exposure can give a show a boost, it can also hurt it. People become saturated and subconsciously stop listening and hearing. In addition, too much exposure creates very high expectations and can lead to disappointment. Poor word of mouth can be created as disappointed theatergoers tell their friends and acquaintances that the show doesn't live up to its promises.

Despite television's effectiveness, the reality is that very few shows advertise over television. Most productions simply do not have the money to do so.

Print

Theatrical advertising is quite different from any other type of advertising and all shows—musical, comedy, or drama—advertise in print. Most producers use one of the four theater advertising agencies. The larger, multifaceted advertising agencies do not have the special astuteness and

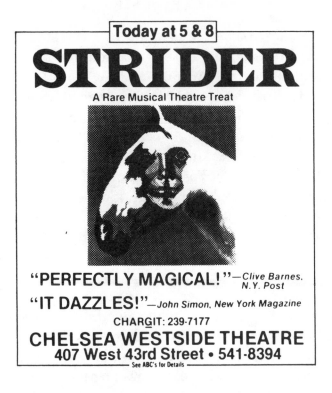

A typical "quote ad," this one from *Strider*. In a quote ad, favorable words or sentences are taken from reviews and published as part of a show's advertisements.

understanding of the specific techniques endemic to theater.

Probably the most important print ad for a production is the "quote ad" that appears immediately after opening. For the quote ad, the most positive lines from the reviews are selected and printed with the critic's name. While always accurate in terms of the actual words used, quote ads are sometimes misleading because they are taken out of context. For instance, a show might get a negative review which contains favorable mention of a certain actor or a certain artistic element in the production. For the quote ad, only the positive quote will be used.

In 1961, producer David Merrick opened a show called *Subways Are For Sleeping*. It got rather mixed reviews, but Merrick decided to run the show, which he did with some success. As a publicity stunt, he decided to run a quote ad and looked in the New York telephone directory to find the names of seven people who bore identical names to the critics on the seven daily newspapers in New York at that time. He invited the seven to see a performance as his guests and then asked them to tell him what they enjoyed about the production.

With his advertising agency, which was, of course, a partner to the joke, he assembled an ad that looked exactly like a typical quote ad with one exception: small photographs of the Merrick "critics" ran alongside their names and quotes. The average reader has no idea what the daily newspaper critics look like and had no way of knowing that the photographs were not those of the regular legitimate critics. The ad actually ran in the first edition of *The New York Times* until someone realized that it was a phony and pulled it from subsequent editions.

Although there is agreement that print advertising doesn't lead to instantaneous ticket buying the way television and radio do, print is important for maintaining a show's recognition factor. If people are thinking of going to the theater, they will often look in the newspaper. If they decide to see a certain show, it is probably because the ad serves as a reminder that this is a show they have wanted to see. One advertising person says: "Theatrical advertising is unique. You cannot give image to a show the way you can to a product. You must take the image from the show and translate it to the public. I really believe that people don't necessarily believe what they see in ads. The quotes are important, but I don't think they sell tickets. People believe much more what they read and see on the editorial pages. People who want to go to the theater look at the entertainment pages of the newspaper. They see your ad and say, 'Oh yes, I heard something about that' and hopefully they'll buy a ticket. The point is that although print probably won't sell a ticket to someone who wouldn't ordinarily buy, if you don't have a print ad, people who are going to buy a theater ticket won't think about your show at all. They'll buy something else."

No one can overestimate the importance of *The New York Times* as an advertising medium for theater. *The New York Times*, particularly the Sunday *Times*, is a national newspaper and reaches a potential audience throughout the nation. For a theatrical production, it provides the outlet for a national advertisement. A large Sunday ad often makes people think that the show is a success, another reason why shows take large ads. The space isn't cheap. A full page costs about $19,000. For any show, the weekly advertising budget just for print is usually about $3,000–$5,000.

Publicity

While the press agent's specific preopening tasks were mentioned in the chapter on rehearsals, the hardest and most creative part of the press agent's job is to generate the kind of excitement and exposure to the production that will motivate people to buy tickets. Since publicity cannot be purchased like advertising, the press agent must somehow make the show or some aspect of it worthy of print, television, or radio exposure.

Newspapers, television, and radio stations are businesses. They are operated for profit. They generate profits from the space and time they sell to advertisers. The more people who buy a newspaper, listen to a radio station, or watch a television channel, the more desirable these media become and the more they can charge their advertisers for time and space.

Aside from the business of printing or broadcasting the daily news, these media therefore must fill their airwaves and pages with the kind of material that interests people. The media constantly conduct surveys to measure the types of programs or feature material that attract audiences and readers.

A big star who appears on a local television talk show will attract a bigger audience than a little-known composer whose off-off-Broadway showcase production is in preview at a small downtown theater. A play like *Romantic Comedy* starring Mia Farrow and Anthony Perkins, which did not get very good reviews, has a better chance of getting publicity than a production like *Strider*, which opened to almost unanimous raves. A publication like *People* magazine is more likely to place Mia Farrow on its cover than Gerald Hiken, the star of *Strider*. Readers will buy *People* to learn about Mia Farrow; they won't buy it to read about Gerald Hiken.

The "Today Show" and "Good Morning America," nationally televised early morning shows, have viewing audiences in the millions. Because they are broadcast from New York, they are the two most desirable shows on which to publicize a Broadway production. Yet the producers of "Today" and "Good Morning America" must make sure (for the sake of their own jobs) that this viewing audience remains in the millions. Therefore they are more likely to feature a celebrity who is a famous star even if the show is mediocre.

So the first thing a press agent must do is to realize the needs of the media and plan a campaign around that. It is the dream of every press agent to have a star or a production which is so famous or important that producers and editors are calling the agent to arrange for guest appearances and interviews. This is very rare. Even when the press agent is handling a hot show, media interest is brief, usually just before the show opens and immediately afterwards. When there is a big star or something unique about the production, a good press agent will not allow all the potential publicity to happen at once. A show constantly needs exposure. The press agent will usually try to delay certain interviews and appearances so that there will be steady exposure over a long term and not just a one-time media explosion, then nothing. One press agent speaks of his work: "The thing I love about theater is that you are there from the beginning. There is something essentially valid about the product. There is a quality that people strive for and a special feeling about what they are doing that doesn't seem to exist in any other field. I'm not saying that the people are nicer or the work is easier. As a matter of fact, you work harder and longer hours in the theater. You are at your office all day long and often at the theater at night.

"But working in the theater has a kind of magic. It's alive! And it is glamorous at times but not as much as most people think. Even bad theater means that someone has taken a risk. It deserves your best effort.

"As the link between the production and the public, you are often blamed if audiences don't come. The producers or the stars think you haven't worked hard for them. There's a saying among press agents that they never get credit when the show is a success and going well but they always get the blame when the show folds. It's hard and often you feel terrible because you're just not getting the breaks. But ultimately theater is something you can feel proud of pushing and promoting. It's not like getting people to buy a different kind of aspirin or another kind of hamburger. The product—the theater—is important and you can feel good about what you do."

Being a press agent used to be easier. There were many more newspapers in New York City and more press space to fill. Nowadays, it is hard to get publicity for a show, especially after it has opened and is settling down for a run. Press agents must be innovative. They must keep trying to come up with different angles—pegs, they are called—to promote shows. As an example, if one of the cast members is a gourmet chef, the press agent will try to get a story on the food pages of a newspaper. If one of the producers is a particularly innovative, stylish dresser or a socialite, the press agent works for a fashion story or mention in the society pages. If a playwright has a particularly fancy or distinguished apartment, the press agent trys to get a home story. The point is that the press agent must always come up with the peg, the idea that will make the story interesting and attractive to the media.

Stunts

One of the things press agents do, particularly for long-running plays, is to try to develop stunts. *Grease* annually placed a Christmas tree on a small pedestrian island between Broadway and Seventh Avenue, directly opposite Times Square. Each year, there was an official lighting ceremony with the cast of *Grease* in attendance. The event usually generated press coverage. The newspapers sent photographers and, sometimes, television stations camera crews to film the event. Of course, *Grease* was always mentioned.

Even lesser-known shows attempt stunts. At each performance of Sam Shepard's *Buried Child*, mounds of carrots and corn were used on stage. The show's press agent decided to donate the discarded vegetables to the New York City Police Department's mounted horse patrol unit. With the Police Department's cooperation, a ceremony was performed outside the theater and the cast of *Buried Child* officially donated the vegetables to the police horses. Five horses were brought to the theater especially for the occasion. The *New York Post* sent a photographer and a picture appeared the next day.

When you see a picture of such an event, read an interview with a celebrity, see a name mentioned in a gossip column, or hear someone on a radio or television talk show, it is almost certain that a press agent arranged it. Most of the time, the press agent has worked hard to get the break, especially if it is for a show that has been running for a while. When it comes to stunts, the press agents are in a high state of anxiety. They have not only thought up and lined up the stunt, they have sent all the newspapers, wire services, and television stations a photo tip—a brief summary of the details of the event, describing the specific photo opportunity.

On the day of the event, the press agent starts calling, asking the media if they will be sending camera crews or a photographer. Usually, unless the press agent is acting as a spokesperson for a real news event, the question never gets answered. There are limited camera crews and photographers available at any one time. Their highest priority is to cover real news stories. Often, a press agent purposely picks a time when there is little chance of another event's occurring. It would be absurd to arrange a stunt on the day the president of the United States comes to New York. All available crews would be covering the president. In any case, press agents never know for sure whether the stunt will get coverage. It is a time of tremendous tension and stomach grinding as press agents and participants wait to see if a photographer or television crew will appear. However, when the event appears on television during the evening news or in the newspaper the next day, it is a wonderful feeling. Not only has the stunt worked, the public has been reminded that the show is still there.

Tickets, Runs, and National Tours

Tickets

Assuming that the show is successful and the advertising and promotion are attracting audiences, how do people buy tickets?

Each Broadway theater has a box office. It is staffed by the house treasurer and his assistants. Until fairly recently, people could purchase tickets for a Broadway production by going to the theater's box office in person and paying for the seats in cash or ordering tickets through the mail, paying by personal check and enclosing some proof of identification. The third alternative was to use the services of a ticket broker. Ticket brokers still exist, maintaining storefront shops throughout the Broadway area and in New York's major hotels. They receive a certain allotment of seats for each show's performance and charge a $3.00 service fee. This figure is fixed by law. Many businesses and individuals maintain accounts with ticket brokers. Ticket brokers can sometimes obtain seats to hit shows on short notice. But most frequently brokers do this only for regular and therefore preferred customers. The man on the street cannot expect to walk into a broker and ask for two tickets

The facade of Liberty Theater Tickets, one of the licensed ticket brokers located in the Broadway area. Ticket sales by brokers account for approximately 40% of all tickets sold. *Photo by Roger Greenawalt*

to tonight's performance of the hottest musical on Broadway and expect to get them.

Today, however, there are many other ways of obtaining tickets to Broadway productions. As a result, the number of people attending the Broadway theater is increasing each year. The League of New York Theatres and Producers annually issues statistics on theater attendance, as does the show business weekly newspaper, *Variety*. During the 1978–79 season, $136 million was spent on theater tickets; 9.8 million people attended theatrical performances. According to *Variety*, during the 1977–78 season, $104 million was spent, with 8.6 million people attending the theater.

Theatergoers can now order tickets by phone through Chargit or go to Ticketron locations in New York City and throughout the nation. Purchasers can pay by cash or charge tickets to a credit card, either American Express, Diners Club, VISA, or MasterCard. The tickets are picked up at the theater at the time of the performance if they are purchased through Chargit. If purchased at a Ticketron location, the tickets are printed out at the time of purchase. It is not unlikely that in the future individual box offices will sell tickets to all Broadway productions instead of only those playing in their theaters.

At the present time, the Shubert Organization is computerizing ticket sales for productions playing in its theaters. In a project expected to cost in excess of $6 million, all tickets to shows playing in Shubert houses will be sold via computer terminals. Eventually, this system will be linked with the Chargit and Ticketron computer systems. This will allow anyone throughout the nation to buy tickets to a Broadway show and know, at the moment of purchase, what seat locations are available for the performance.

One fairly recent innovation in ticket buying has been the TKTS Booth. Called "the Booth," it is run under the management of the Theatre Development Fund. TDF is a nonprofit organization, founded in 1967 to stimulate the production of worthwhile plays in the commercial theater. Today, it subsidizes low-cost admissions to both commercial and not-for-profit theater.

The Booth, with two locations, one in the Times Square area and the other near Wall Street, sells tickets at half price. Each day, some productions send an allotment of tickets to the Booth for that day's performance. The names

TKTS (Tickets) Booth, operated by the Theatre Development Fund, is one of the reasons why theater attendance has been steadily increasing each year. Each day, certain shows send tickets to the Booth which are then sold at half price for that day's performance. The lines at the Booth in the Broadway area (another is located downtown in the Wall Street area) are usually very long, reflecting the popularity of New York City's most glamorous industry. *Photo by Roger Greenawalt*

of the shows with available seats are posted at the Booth.

Since its inception in 1974, the Booth has sold more than 5 million tickets to Broadway shows, off-Broadway shows, music and dance events. The Booth has also been responsible for a mini-industry that offers employment to numerous unemployed actors and others who are trying to get into the theater. Most producers hire people to hand out fliers about their show to those standing on line at the Booth. Those handing out the fliers often try to convince potential buyers to purchase tickets to the shows they represent. Their selling techniques would be the envy of any salesman. When the weather is good, the Booth is headquarters for New York street musicians and performers who entertain those waiting on line. Although the lines can be long, waiting on line at the Booth is often fun and entertaining.

The Theatre Development Fund also helps ticket sales through its ticket subsidy program. TDF purchases large blocks of tickets at a substantial discount, which it then offers to its membership mailing list. The TDF list is restricted to students, teachers, union members, retired persons, the clergy, professionals in the performing arts, and members of the armed forces. This particular service of TDF has done much to allow certain shows to build up an audience and maintain themselves through those first often difficult weeks. Such hits as *Sweeney Todd*, *Elephant Man*, and *On Golden Pond* have been the recipients of TDF subsidy aid.

"Two-fers"—two for the price of one—are also used to sell theater tickets. Toward the end of a run, shows frequently need audiences. Two-fers may be found on the counters of various stores and offices throughout the metropolitan area.

A variation of the two-fer are tickets sent to schools and nonprofit organizations. These organizations are offered tickets at specially reduced rates. The cost of the mailing is assumed by the production company. Reduced-rate tickets are not only for the end of a show's run; frequently, producers arrange for school mailings before the show has even opened. This is obviously done when the production is thought to have some appeal to students. Such tickets help guarantee an audience while the show has time to build and generate full-paying customers through word of mouth, advertising, and publicity.

There are, in addition, many groups that purchase large numbers of seats in advance to Broadway productions. Subscription organizations such as "Play of the Month" or theater clubs sponsored by stores and even certain publications offer theatergoers the opportunity to attend the theater on a regular basis. For a small fee, theatergoers can join one of these subscription plans. As long as people are willing to plan their theatergoing fairly far in advance, they can be assured of good seats in desirable locations for most of the top Broadway shows.

Among the most important ticket sales organizations are those that handle groups and theater parties. They are, for the most part, run and staffed by women known in the business as theater party ladies. Theater party ladies are ticket brokers. But, unlike the ticket brokers who maintain walk-in facilities on the street and sell one-to-one on a per performance basis, the theater party ladies purchase blocks of tickets at a discount. They are paid a commission by the producer. They then sell the tickets to organizations that, in turn, sell these seats at a higher price to their members. The price rise is a means of raising funds for charity or the organization.

Groups and benefits are very important to a show. Often the theater party ladies make their "buys" well in advance of a show's opening. Producers want these groups in their theaters. Frequently, producers even hold preopening auditions, very much like the backers' auditions, to try to interest the theater party ladies in their shows. Actors often say that they don't like performing for benefit groups; they feel that all too often the audience has come to the theater more to see one another than to watch a show. However, parties can do much to build a production's advance sales. They can also make survival difficult for a production which opens to bad or mixed reviews as the theater party ladies can cancel previously booked groups and benefits. Basically, though, when a show has parties booked before opening, it means people believe the production a possible winner. This can be a strong selling point for a producer who is still trying to raise money.

There is another way of obtaining tickets, but it is available only to a fortunate few. This is having access to house seats. House seats are the best locations in the theater. They are allocated to certain people, including the press agent, general manager, producer, and advertising agency. Often stars and key artistic personnel also hold house seats. The box office is not permitted to sell those tickets to the general public until twenty-four or in some cases forty-eight hours before the performance. If you know someone in the production or are in the theater, you can call one of the people holding house seats and if the seats are available you can buy them.

When ticket sales are not going well, there are two things that producers can do with the assistance of the box office: paper and dress the house. Papering the house is the term used when tickets are given away. This is frequently done during previews or when a show has opened to bad reviews and is planning to close within the week. For the morale of the performers, and to improve the atmosphere for those who have paid (no one wants to sit in an empty house), an effort is made to get an audience into the house, even a non-paying one.

Dressing the house is the assigning of seats in such a way as to make the theater look fuller than it actually is. If a show is doing poor or only adequate business, a good treasurer will sell tickets so that most areas of the orchestra have people sitting in them. A house that holds 1,000 people but has a small audience would look fairly empty if all the ticket holders were assigned seats in one section. Dressing the house to make the theater look fuller is important because you don't want an audience leaving the theater and telling people that the house was almost empty.

Keeping the Show Fresh

In addition to making sure that the name of the show remains alive and before the public through advertising and publicity, it is very important to make sure that the show remains alive on stage as well. There are some people who make it a point never to see a show after the first few months of its run. They feel that often, with the passage of time, the quality of excitement, the almost palpable tension that is part of a theatrical event evaporates.

This can be a real problem. A Broadway show plays eight performances a week—a rigorous schedule. For the principals, this can be physically and emotionally exhausting. For the chorus, the singers and dancers, or those in smaller supporting roles, it is frequently a struggle simply to avoid performing by rote and just speaking the lines.

Ordinarily, the stage manager or production supervisor has the responsibility of maintaining the quality of the performances. One stage manager talks of this: "When the show opens, I take over from the director and start working with the actors in a directorial way. How well this is done depends upon one's understanding of what the director has done. I ask myself questions—'Why has he staged things a certain way? How did he get the results he did?' You really should understand the directorial process and it is very important to have a good rapport with the director.

"Usually I don't call the show on Tuesday or Wednesday matinee. I sit and watch. If I see a trend—a movement becomes a little too broad or a certain sloppiness—I give a note to the actor. Usually actors are very responsive to notes, even stars. Some, of course, challenge me and sometimes there is a lot of discussion back and forth as an actor tells me why he was doing what I had questioned. If there's really a problem, we'll go out for a drink after the show and talk about it."

The problem of keeping a show fresh is particularly evident in small productions in which the interplay and ensemble acting between the characters is the primary focus of the production. The audience cannot be lulled by a big singing or dance number. *Ain't Misbehavin'* was sharply criticized in Liz Smith's nationally syndicated newspaper column about a year and a half into its run. Noting talk that the production was becoming sloppy and losing its energy, Ms. Smith mentioned that understudies were appearing in place of the principals with a frequency much greater than average. With a cast of six, this was important. The producers of *Ain't Misbehavin'* took note and immediately attempted to correct the situation. That kind of public notice is the worst publicity a show can have. Occasionally, one of the New York City daily newspapers or *Variety* will rereview a production after it has run a long time. This is a way of keeping all the company on their toes although, most frequently, it is done when a new star enters the show.

Some producers are rigorous about making sure that their shows stay fresh. The producers of *Grease* insisted that the director or choreographer see the show every three months. In addition, since *Grease* became almost a small industry in itself, its producers devised an unofficial training period for cast replacements. Usually, replacements for the Broadway company of *Grease* were selected from one of the road companies. This provided an impetus for the road cast members to keep their performances in shape as most would rather have been on Broadway than on the road. It also gave the *Grease* producers the opportunity to pick the very best actors as replacements.

There are some actors and actresses who refuse to stay with a production for more than six months or a year at most. They recognize that if they did, some of their enthusiasm would be lost. Angela Lansbury, star of *Gypsy* and *Sweeney Todd*, has stated that she will not stay with a musical for more than a year or a straight play for more than six months. This is not because she, like some big-name stars, wants to do other more lucrative projects. Miss Lansbury is concerned about her own capacity to maintain her role and performance after that point. On the other hand, some actors are very happy in the same role for long periods of time, feeling that they never exhaust the possibilities inherent in a role they care about.

Few actors or actresses have the dedication of the late Rosalind Russell. In Chicago with the company of the play *Bell, Book and Candle*, her final performance was on a Saturday night. But she was not happy with the production and that morning, prior to the matinee, she asked for a refresher rehearsal. Obviously, much of the spirit of the production has to do with how the cast members feel about themselves and each other. A happy cast usually works better together. Feuds, which hardly ever spread beyond the confines of backstage, do sometimes spill over onto the stage, to the detriment of the production.

Sometimes, replacements must be cast on the basis of meshing with the company's acting style. An acting company, particularly one that has been together from the start, develops a style. If replacements are unable to adapt to that style it can be destructive to company morale, to say nothing of the performance. An acting company becomes a small family, developing unique ways of coping with the joys and strains of being so close. Just as it would be virtually impossible for an outsider immediately to understand and take a part in the subtle chemistry of a real family, it is difficult to enter an acting company without developing a sensitivity and concern about how the company works together.

Road Companies

When a production has been successful on Broadway, the producers often form a national road company. Road companies are usually booked into theaters across the nation by a New York–based booking agency, the International Booking Organization (IBO). Sometimes, however, the general manager's office, under the supervision of the producer, arranges the schedule. The following is a typical schedule. It is for the 1980–81 national tour of *Camelot*, in which Richard Burton repeated his starring role.

June 9–28:	pre-Broadway stand in Toronto
July 1–August 24:	New York State Theatre, New York City
August 27–September 21:	Arie Crown, Chicago

September 30–October 12:	State Fair Auditorium, Dallas
October 22–November 23:	Theatre of the Performing Arts, Miami
November 25–December 14:	Saenger Performing Arts Center, New Orleans
December 17–March 8:	Golden Gate Theatre, San Francisco
March 11–June 7:	Pantages, Los Angeles

Usually, a national company is formed either during or following a successful Broadway run. Work normally begins on the company about three months before the tour sets out, although actual theater bookings often begin a year before. Traditionally, the original director is asked to direct the first national company, and often the members of the New York company are asked if they want to go on the road. If the show is still playing on Broadway, replacements must be cast for those who decide to go. The director must often restage the New York company because of the many replacements.

A national company is big business. For a musical, the potential grosses can be well over $200,000 a week. Shows are reviewed in each city and, of course, reviews influence out-of-town ticket sales much the same way that they do in New York. It is true that a national company has a reputation that precedes it, unlike a new show opening on Broadway. It is also true that a national company is not a second-class citizen in the theater. The goal is to make that company equal to the Broadway company.

Name stars increasingly go out on the road. This is in part because salaries have increased to the point where a star is often guaranteed a payment of $25,000 to $35,000 a week, plus expenses. Obviously, a national name helps draw an audience. But the accompanying expenses also mean that a show must do well out of town in order to make money. Angela Lansbury went on the road with *Sweeney Todd*; Alexis Smith in *The Best Little Whorehouse in Texas*; Richard Kiley in *Man of La Mancha*, and Jackie Gleason in *Sly Fox*. A national company is quite literally a first-class production, with the prestige of a Broadway production that tours.

As on Broadway, ticket sales mean everything. Often, national tours are booked into cities to tie in with local theater subscriptions. This means that the producer can be fairly confident that the production will have an audience. However, since touring companies often play a theater only for a couple of weeks, it is always necessary to build ticket sales for a show. A touring show is expected to have an advance before it enters a city. An out-of-town show that is playing a nine-week limited engagement does not have the time or economic resources to take four weeks of that run to build its audience.

The person responsible for ticket sales is the road or touring agent. This person is a press agent, a member of ATPAM. There are some press agent ATPAM members who spend most of their working life on the road. Others go out on the road only at certain times. Reasons differ: there is no work in New York, they feel like going on the road for a while, or they have become so involved with the New York production that their knowledge is indispensable for the show's success on the road.

Road agents function as advance people. They go on contract four weeks before the show begins out of town and immediately set out for the first stop on the tour. The road agent handles the out-of-town advertising. Sometimes what works in New York doesn't work out of town. The logo for *Ain't Misbehavin'* on Broadway was a photograph of the cast; an entirely new logo had to be designed for the touring company because the New York cast was not going on the road. It is the road agent's responsibility to coordinate all the out-of-town advertising, either working with the New York–based agency or the local advertising agency hired for each city's engagement. Sometimes the New York advertising agency places the ads out of town and buys the radio and television time. However, in some cities, the local agency can get much better rates. It is the responsibility of the road agent to make these decisions and suggest the best schedules and outlets for advertising.

The road agent must also generate publicity and promotion. Out of town, the road agent often actually visits the newspapers and meets editors and critics. Just as New York press agents know most of the New York theatrical press, the road agent is expected to have a relationship with the out-of-town press and to excite them about the production. The judgment and good will of media people are very important to the success of the national company.

The road agent also ends up doing a lot of things that are not strictly publicity and advertising. One road agent speaks of the work: "I am there to protect the production. As road agent, you are the only person who actually sees the city before the show gets there. I am the only person physically present. I size up the entire situation and continually report back to New York.

"For instance, when I am taking a show on the road, one of the first things I do is sit down with the stage manager and the company manager. They will be traveling with the show. I get a list from the stage manager of what he needs to know. That can be things like how many dressing rooms there are in the theater, where they are located, how much room there is for the sound board and equipment, whether or not certain sets that are being constructed by the theater's crew are coming along and staying in budget . . . . For the company manager, I often have to check the hotels, track down furnished apartments because a lot of people prefer not to sleep in hotels every night. I have to line up doctors in case anyone gets sick. If there are children, I hire schoolteachers and tutors as the law is that children must be taught, even on the road. I even look for restaurants that can serve dinner after the show. In a city like Boston, that's not hard. But in a place like Cleveland, it really is hard to find a place that is open at 11:00 P.M. where the cast can eat. All that is very important.

"I really try to smooth the way for the entire production and that includes living as well as performing. I even scout out dance classes or health clubs so people can work out. It's a lot to do in four weeks and don't forget, I'm alone most of the time. Occasionally, if it's a real complicated show, the producer will pay to have the carpenter or electrician come in in advance to check things out. But usually, it's up to me and all the time, I am trying to get those seats sold. It's exhilarating because you are completely independent but it can also be lonely. But there really is a lure of the road."

The road agent sets up publicity appearances and interviews which will start as soon as the production arrives. Sometimes, a star is flown in in advance for guest appearances and interviews. The road agent usually remains in town for the opening but often leaves immediately to "advance" the next city.

At this point, much of the traditional functions of the

press agent are assumed by the company manager and stage manager. One agent says: "On the road, everyone helps everyone else. It is one of the traditions that the company manager and the stage manager take over for me the same way I do for them when I'm advancing the show."

Company managers and stage managers often oversee the interviews and appearances set up by press agents. They make sure the cast members keep dates and engagements, often accompanying them, and see to it that costumes are delivered to events or television appearances in time—in New York usually the job of the press agent. All of this mutual cooperation is part of the protocol of the road.

What is fun about the road is its unpredictability. All road agents have stories about the road. One press agent advancing a show traveled with her small dog. As she walked into an out-of-town newspaper with her dog in a carpet bag, the dog leaped out of the bag. A story was written about the dog who was advancing the show. The dog ended up the focus of stories in nearly every city the show played.

Another road agent was traveling with a European circus. He was the only English-speaking person. A circus horse became sick in a small town in Pennsylvania. The agent had to take the temperature of the horse and tell the veterinarian on the other end of the telephone what it was.

One of the agents advancing the road company of *Hair* appeared on local radio. Ordinarily, press agents do not appear on television or radio, but sometimes, they are the only available spokespeople for the show. It was a question-and-answer call-in show. A tour of *Hair* was not easy to handle. Few hotels wanted a band of hippies, and it was also an election year and many local politicians decided to generate press for themselves by trying to ban such an irreverent show from their city. One of the questions asked over the radio station concerned the brief moment of nudity at the end of the first act. The road agent pointed out that there were actually so many costumes that the production traveled with its own washing machine and dryer. This fact became the source of several out-of-town features that not only provided insight as to how a production travels but managed to help defuse the issue about *Hair* being a nude show, which, of course, it wasn't.

For the cast, being on the road is special. One cast member who traveled with a big musical says: "I think that everyone in a road company simply has to get along together. We become each other's families. There's an incredible kind of spirit. We're all supportive of one another. We're all in this together and it's a fun and good time. There's always someone to go out with and usually someone is having a party after the show.

"Of course, living out of hotel rooms is hard. You don't stay in the best hotels in town. People are never happy with the hotel but you really can't afford anything else. And it seems traditional to complain about that. When I'm in a town, the first thing I do is find a dance class or at least someplace I can exercise. That's really important to me. I sightsee and explore the city. You sleep late usually so there's not as much time as you'd think to really explore. By the time you take care of laundry, go to brush-up rehearsals, eat meals . . . that's pretty much the day. And then you perform at night and at matinees. So, the time goes really quickly."

Going out on the road is one of the unique experiences in the theater. It is always tiring. The constant traveling, restaurant food, and hotel rooms can get demoralizing. It is difficult to make new friendships because the schedule of the theater is different from most other people's. But the road is an exhilarating time and always memorable. In the theater, there is always the show. But, on the road, there is something else as well—an intensity, a closeness and support that are the essence of theatrical life.

Glossary

ABC's: Small advertisements placed in daily newspapers which, alphabetically by title, list current Broadway and off-Broadway shows, their performance schedules and ticket prices.

Actors' Equity Association: The union for all performers in the legitimate theater in the United States and Canada.

Angel: An individual who invests money in a commercial theatrical production; a backer.

ATPAM: Association of Theatrical Press Agents and Managers. The union to which press agents, company managers, and house managers belong.

Backer: An investor in a commercial theatrical production.

Backers' audition: A gathering to which prospective investors in a production are invited to hear selections from the projected play or musical. It is usually held in an apartment or private room of a restaurant. The plot is described, some musical selections performed, and the producers describe and distribute the production's offering circular and limited partnership agreement.

Billing: The ranking of all names associated with a production. It is determined by contracts signed between producer and actors and artistic personnel. Billing determines not only the order of names but size, position, and boldness of type and when the names must appear on materials associated with the production.

Blocking: The physical movements of actors prescribed by the director.

Book: In the musical theater, the script or story.

Break-even: The sum of money at which the gross weekly box office receipts equal the production's weekly operating costs.

Bus and truck: A production that travels from town to town, sometimes playing only a single engagement in each place. The actors travel by bus and the scenery and other equipment by truck.

Call board: A bulletin board placed by the stage door on which sign-in sheets, rehearsal schedules, closing notice, and all other information for the cast are posted.

Casting: The process of selecting actors and actresses for the roles in a production.

Casting director: Someone retained by the producer to find actors for the roles in a production. The casting director brings suitable actors to those who will actually do the hiring—the producer, playwright, and director.

Capitalization: The sum of money required to produce a show.

Capitalization budget: Also called production budget; the budget that contains an itemized breakdown of each expenditure necessary to mount a production. It includes all of the production's expenses through opening and is included in the offering circular given to potential investors.

Close booking: The practice among theater owners of lining up another production to take occupancy of their theater if and when the current production occupying the theater closes.

Closing notice: An announcement posted on the call board that states the date on which a production will close. Actors' Equity and the other theatrical unions require that a closing notice be posted the week before the production closes. The producer can take a closing notice down and continue to run the show. However, the posting of the notice releases all personnel from any contractual obligation to remain with the production.

Company manager: The producer's day-to-day representative at the theater. A member of ATPAM, the company manager is employed by the general manager and oversees the production's daily financial and business affairs. The company manager is present for all performances and signs the daily box office statement.

Contract: A written agreement between two or more people, enforceable by law. In the theater, contracts determine salaries and fees; employment conditions; billing; location of dressing rooms; and often other perquisites for actors, such as transportation to and from the theater and dressers to help prepare for the show.

Contract house: A theater that is commited to hiring a minimum number of musicians regardless of whether they are actually needed.

Credits: The listing, at the end of the program or playbill, of all the suppliers who have provided props, scenery, and other materials used in a production.

Critic: A theater reviewer.

Dramatists Guild: The professional society that prescribes the minimum terms of the agreement (contract) signed between producer and playwright or, in the case of a musical, the agreements between the producer and the librettist, composer and lyricist.

Dressing the house: The box office practice of selling tickets in such a way that, when patrons are seated, the theater looks fuller than it actually is.

End money: Also called last money; the last portion of money needed to finance a future production so that it is fully capitalized and can begin production.

Favored nations clause: A clause in an actor's contract guaranteeing that his or her salary and billing are equal to those of other actors in the production. Billing is alphabetical and appears in the same size and boldness of type. If another actor is signed to a contract providing for a higher salary or better billing, the favored nations contracts are automatically adjusted so that everyone receives the same salary and billing.

Four-wall contract: A rental agreement for a theater in which the producer pays a fixed sum for rent and all of the theater's operating expenses.

Freezing a performance: The point, before opening, when the director stops making changes in a production in order to allow actors to perform without having to adjust to new direction.

Front money: All funds required to develop a future production; the funds used during preproduction until the actual production company is formed and the show's financing is complete.

Front of the House: In the theater itself, the entire area with the exception of the stage and backstage areas. Also used for the outside of the theater, specifically the marquee and the cases in which pictures and the houseboard are mounted. "Decorating the front of the house" is the term used for placing materials outside the theater.

General partner: The producer of the show who makes the day-to-day decisions about the operations of the production; the name the public associates with the show. General partners ordinarily receive 50 percent of all profits realized from a production.

Gross: The total amount of money taken in at the theater box office for a performance or for the week.

Half hour: The alert given to the cast by the stage manager one half hour before the performance. The cast must be at the theater by half hour.

Hot ticket: A smash hit for which seats are in heavy demand.

Houseboard: A board mounted in front of the theater on which the name of the production and all actors and artistic personnel who receive billing are listed in the correct order, size, and type as determined by contractual agreements and union regulations.

House manager: The theater owner's representative at the theater who is in charge of the day-to-day operation of the theater. The house manager is a member of ATPAM.

House seats: Seats in the best section of the theater that are reserved in limited number for certain people connected with the production, such as the press agent, general manager, stars, etc. Those holding house seats can release them to individuals they choose, who must then take a house seat order form to the box office, usually twenty-four hours before the specified performance, and pay for the tickets.

Impresario: A person who represents or sponsors an entertainment event. The term is used most frequently in the sphere of opera, concerts, dance, and other musical performances.

Industrial show: A production sponsored by a company or business to describe its products. Industrial shows are usually performed at trade conventions and gatherings and are designed to bolster employee enthusiasm and performance. They provide a lot of work for actors.

Ingenue: A naive young woman; in the theater, often used to describe a role suitable for young and upcoming actress.

Interim booking: The practice of booking a production to occupy a theater with the understanding that the show will have to vacate by a certain date as another production has been promised the theater.

Joint venture: The joining together of two or more producers to mount a production.

Joint venture agreement: A legally binding contract between coproducers stating the rights and obligations of each.

Limited partnership: The most common means of producing a show. A limited partnership production company consists of general partners and limited partners. The general partners are the name producers and make all the artistic and financial decisions. They share in 50 percent of any profits realized from the production. The limited partners are the cash investors. Their sole obligation is to invest the agreed-upon sum and their sole liability is limited to the amount of their investment. They share, according to their individual investment, the other 50 percent of any profits.

Limited partnership agreement: The document signed between general partner and limited partner creating the limited partnership production company that will produce the play.

Lip Syncing: Moving one's mouth to prerecorded music and only pretending to sing or speak. This is done most frequently in the theater when performers must do vigorous movements while singing.

Logo: A graphic symbol or design used by a production for display advertisements, posters, and front of the house.

Middle house: A theater with a capacity of no more than 499 seats located in the Broadway theater district as defined by the various theatrical unions. This is within the confines of Fifth and Ninth Avenues from 34th to 56th Street and of Fifth Avenue and the Hudson River from 56th to 72d Street. Middle houses are also called 499 houses. As of 1980, there are four: the Rialto, the Playhouse, the Century, and the Princess.

Net profits: Funds paid to investors after recoupment (the point at which the original investment is paid back). The difference between gross box office receipts and the production's weekly operating expenses at that point represents net profit.

Notices: A production's reviews.

Nut: What it costs to run a production each week; weekly operating expenses.

Off-Broadway: As defined by the theatrical unions, a theater with a capacity of no more than 499 seats located outside the geographical areas between Fifth and Ninth Avenues from 34th Street to 56th Street and between Fifth Avenue and the Hudson River from 56th Street to 72d Street. Most off-Broadway theaters have a maximum capacity of 299 seats and are often referred to as "299 houses."

Off-off-Broadway: What off-Broadway used to be before it became part of the commercial theater, operating under guidelines established by the theatrical unions. Although Actors' Equity under its Showcase Code mandates the number of performances that can take place each week and guarantees actors and artistic personnel certain benefits if an off-off-Broadway show moves to off-Broadway or Broadway, off-off-Broadway offers theater that is often too experimental for the commercial theater and provides an arena for actors, playwrights, and other creative people to perform and test their work in a noncommercial setting.

Offering circular: A document given to potential investors in a production that contains all relevant information an investor would want to know about the prospective show. It includes biographical material on the producers and artistic personnel and a complete budget and financial breakdown.

Option: The agreement between a producer and playwright or the holder of the rights to a play or source material which gives the producer the exclusive rights to produce the property within a specified amount of time.

Overcall: An additional sum of money, over the initial investment, that a limited partner may be asked to invest in financing a production. An overcall usually amounts to 10 percent of each limited partner's original investment. The amount of a possible overcall is stated in the offering circular and included in the limited partnership agreement signed between investor and producer.

Papering the house: The practice of giving away free tickets to a production, usually done during preview performances or when a show is about to close in order to prevent actors from having to play to what might otherwise be a nearly empty theater.

Penalty house: A theater that hires musicians only when it needs them for a show. The musicians are paid a higher wage than those working for a contract house.

Photo call: The time set for actors to pose in costume and on the set for photographs of the production. The theatrical unions require that written notification be given twenty-four hours in advance.

Press agent: A member of ATPAM; the person who publicizes the show and oversees the entire marketing, advertising, and promotion of a production.

Press tickets: Free tickets for seats located in the best section of the theater; technically designated for legitimate members of the working press.

Property: The basic work optioned by a producer from which a production will be developed.

Quote ad: A print advertisement in which favorable quotations from reviews are printed.

Recoupment: The point at which the production makes back its total capitalization. The investors receive the amount of their investment plus any overcall. Any funds after that become profit.

Regional theater: Established theater companies throughout the nation that present an ongoing season of productions. Most are not-for-profit theater subsidized by foundation, state, and local government grants. Many shows that come to Broadway are first produced at regional theaters.

Repertory: A theater that produces several plays in one season in which the same group of actors perform, rotating parts, so that in one play an actor may play the lead but in another he may play a smaller role. In a repertory company the group of actors work together on all productions.

Road: The entire nation, outside of Manhattan, traveled by shows; "taking the show on the road" or "going on the road" is traveling with a production as it tours the nation, playing in cities other than New York.

Royalty: A percentage of a production's weekly box office receipts given to certain people affiliated with the production.

Second night: Technically, the performance following opening night; the performance to which the second-string critics and press are invited (those with weekly newspapers, monthly magazines, certain radio and television shows). Second night can be several performances to which these press people and critics are invited.

Session fee: A sum of money paid for a specific service usually performed in a film or recording studio and not before an audience; the term is most frequently used for payments given for commercials or recording sessions.

Showcase: A production, usually mounted in an off-off-Broadway theater, in which actors perform primarily for the purpose of being seen by those in the business who can help them obtain work—casting directors, agents, and producers. These performances come under the Showcase Code as prescribed by Actors' Equity.

Souvenir book: A program sold in the lobby of a theater. It is more elaborate than the playbill, which is distributed for free, and includes color photographs and additional information about the production, its actors and artistic personnel.

Standby: An actor who is hired to be available to assume the role of a principal actor, usually a star. A standby must call in a half hour before curtain time and be within a specified agreed-upon distance from the theater. If a standby does not have to go on, he or she need not be at the theater although a standby must attend special rehearsals at least once a week.

Stock and amateur rights: Also known as second-class rights; the permission to mount performances of a production in summer theater, stock, college and university productions, and amateur groups.

Stock theater: A theatrical organization which produces its own shows and doesn't book traveling attractions or touring companies.

Stop clause: A provision in the contract between theater owner and producer that gives the theater owner the right to evict the production if it fails to gross an agreed-upon sum for two consecutive weeks.

Straight play: A nonmusical production.

Subsidiary rights: All of the possible uses of a production other than the stage and first-class touring companies. Subsidiary rights include movies, television productions, recordings, amateur and stock productions, bus and truck, etc.

Swing house: A theater that can accommodate either musicals or straight plays.

Theater party: Also called a benefit, a group of theatergoers who attend a production as part of a fund-raising event for an organization. The organization purchases a block of tickets at a discount rate and then sells the tickets for more money than the purchase price. The difference between the initial purchase price and what the theatergoer pays goes to the organization for which funds are being raised and can be deducted from income taxes as a charitable contribution.

Tony Awards: Short for Antoinette Perry Awards, the Broadway theater's most prestigious awards. They are announced and presented each June over a special national telecast. The Tony is named in honor of the late Antoinette Perry, former chairman of the board and secretary of the American Theater Wing, a nonprofit service and educational organization under whose auspices the Tony Awards are presented.

Trades: Show business publications that publish information pertinent to individuals working in the entertainment industry. Popular publications include *Backstage*, *Variety*, and *Show Business*.

Understudy: An actor who substitutes for another actor who is unable to perform. An understudy performs a smaller featured or chorus role in the company. Understudies attend special rehearsals at least once a week.

Walking musician (walker): A walking musician simply collects his or her check and "walks away" without having to perform.

Bibliography

Atkinson, Brooks. *Broadway*. New York: Macmillan, 1970.

Aldrich, Richard Stoddard. *Gertrude Lawrence as Mrs. A*. New York: Greystone Press, 1954.

Bacall, Lauren. *By Myself*. New York: Alfred A. Knopf, 1978.

Bentley, Eric. *What Is Theatre?* New York: Atheneum, 1968.

Farber, Donald C. *From Option to Opening*. New York: DBS Publications, 1970.

Gard, Robert E., Marston Balch, and Pauline Temkin. *Theatre in America*. Madison, Wis.: Dembar Educational Research Services, Inc., 1968.

Goldman, William. *The Season*. New York: Harcourt, Brace & World, 1969.

Greenberger, Howard. *The Off-Broadway Experience*. Englewood Cliffs, N.J.: Prentice-Hall, 1971.

Gottfried, Martin. *Broadway Musicals*. New York: Harry N. Abrams, 1979.

Guernsey, Jr., Otis L., ed. *The Best Plays of 1976-1977*. New York: Dodd, Mead, 1977.

_____. *The Best Plays of 1977-1978*. New York: Dodd, Mead, 1979.

_____. *The Best Plays of 1978-1979*. New York: Dodd, Mead, 1980.

Hart, Moss. *Act One*. New York: Random House, 1959.

Hartnoll, Phyllis, ed. *The Concise Oxford Companion to the Theatre*. Great Britain: Oxford University Press, 1972.

Harrison, Rex. *Rex*. New York: William Morrow, 1975.

Henderson, Mary C. *The City and the Theatre*. Clifton, N.J.: James T. White & Company, 1973.

Higham, Charles. *Kate: The Life of Katherine Hepburn*. New York: W. W. Norton, 1975.

Langley, Stephen. *Theatre Management in America*. New York: Drama Book Specialists, 1974.

Lewis, R.W. *Edith Wharton: A Biography*. New York: Harper & Row, 1975.

Little, Stuart W., and Arthur Cantor. *The Playmakers*. New York: E.P. Dutton, 1971.

Logan, Joshua. *Josh*. New York: Delacorte Press, 1976.

_____. *Movie Stars, Real People, and Me*. New York: Delacorte Press, 1978.

Massey, Raymond. *A Hundred Different Lives*. Boston: Little, Brown, 1979.

Mozel, Tad, with Gertrude Macy. *Leading Lady: The World and Theatre of Katherine Cornell*. Boston: Atlantic, Little, Brown, 1978.

Rodgers, Richard. *Musical Stages*. New York: Random House, 1975.

Russell, Rosalind, and Chris Chase. *Life Is a Banquet*. New York: Random House, 1977.

Stagg, Jerry. *The Brothers Shubert*. New York: Random House, 1968.

Stevenson, Isabelle, ed. *The Tony Award*. New York: Arno Press, 1975.

Taylor, Theodore. *Jule: The Story of Composer Jule Styne*. New York: Random House, 1979.

Teichmann, Howard C. *George S. Kaufman: An Intimate Portrait*. New York: Atheneum, 1972.

Wharton, Edith. *The Age of Innocence*. New York: Charles Scribner's Sons, 1968 (orig. 1920).

Willis, John, ed. *Theatre World*, vols. 33, 34. New York: Crown Publishers, 1976-1978.

Index